SECOND EDITION

THE

ASSISTANT PRINCIPAL

Leadership
Choices
and
Challenges

Catherine Marshall | Richard M. Hooley

CORWIN PRESS
A SAGE Publications Company
Thousand Oaks, California

For information:

Corwin Press
A Sage Publications Company
2455 Teller Road
Thousand Oaks, California 91320
www.corwinpress.com

Sage Publications Ltd.
1 Oliver's Yard
55 City Road
London EC1Y 1SP
United Kingdom

Sage Publications India Pvt. Ltd.
B-42, Panchsheel Enclave
Post Box 4109
New Delhi 110 017 India

Printed in the United States of America.

This book is printed on acid-free paper.

Library of Congress Cataloging-in-Publication Data

Marshall, Catherine.
The assistant principal : leadership choices and challenges / Catherine Marshall and Richard M. Hooley.—2nd ed.
    p. cm.
Includes bibliographical references and index.
ISBN 0-7619-3151-1 (cloth)—ISBN 0-7619-3152-X (pbk.)
    1. School principals—United States—Case studies. 2. School management and organization—United States. I. Hooley, Richard M. II. Title.
LB2831.92.M37 2006
371.2′012—dc22   2005031691

06 07 08 09 10 9 8 7 6 5 4 3 2 1

Acquiring Editor:	Elizabeth Brenkus
Editorial Assistants:	Desirée Enayati and Candice L. Ling
Typesetter:	C&M Digitals (P) Ltd.
Indexer:	Nara Wood
Cover Designer:	Rose Storey
Graphic Designer:	Lisa Miller

Contents

Preface

The assistant principal's day may include intervening in a heated and violent fight between two eighth graders, chairing a curriculum integration task force, and serving as substitute for the ailing chorus director. What motivates someone to take this varied and variable job? How are the jobs and tasks of assistant principals designed and structured? What training and selection prepare them? Are assistant principals really needed, and if so, for what? Can the job with all of its components, variously interpreted in every district, not to mention every school, even be analyzed using any common understandings?

How can districts and state policies improve the assistant principalship? How can assistant principals take charge of their careers and make theirs a satisfying position? Given the dilemmas and demands, who would want the job? Who would stay in the job? How can principals, policymakers, and preparation programs change to provide better support for them?

The assistant is often ignored and sometimes maligned. The old *Encyclopedia of School Administration and Supervision* (Gorton, Schneider, & Fisher, 1988) in its selection of "administrative roles" does not mention the assistant principal at all. Yet the assistant is often the first person to deal with any immediate challenges in a school, whether curricular or disciplinary.

This book truly values the assistant. After we describe what we know about assistants, we explore how to find and retain people for this role. Research focusing on the position—delineating the particular roles, the processes of selection and socialization, the problems, and the opportunities in the assistantship—sets the context. This book pays attention to unique issues: the challenges facing the person in the entry-level position, the "mop-up" nature of the tasks, the assistant as a gateway to upper administrative mobility, the dependency on

principals and their leadership style, and the particular ambigui-
ties, especially in an era of reform called "accountability," "teacher
empowerment," and "site-based management."

Stray comments and observations piqued our interest in the
assistant principalship. As a public school teacher, Marshall chuck-
led over the middle school students' caricatures of the assistant
principal as a gangster, Nazi, or thug, since the roles of chief disciplinarian and hall patroller have traditionally fallen to the assistant.
Later, as researchers on educational administration careers, we noted
educators' acceptance of the assistantship as a necessary but often
undesirable step up the career ladder (and one that has been difficult
for women and minorities to obtain). We have noted the need to support and motivate assistants in their instructional leadership duties
and their leadership styles. As authors with duties in preparing, promoting, and supporting new entrants to administrative careers
(Marshall as professor of graduate students and Hooley as a district
superintendent), we have watched hundreds entering and moving up
the administrative career hierarchy. We have had fascinating discussions with educators who described their delight in the work and
also their frustration over dilemmas in the assistant principal role.
They describe feeling underpaid and unappreciated by the public
and feeling a sense of helplessness over seemingly intractable societal problems—family breakups, poverty, poor health and nutrition,
racism, drugs, violence—that spill over into the schools. Assistant
principals are on the front line dealing with these problems. They
know their work is important!

Finally, as scholars reviewing the literature, we noted an abun-
dance of material on superintendents and principals but little on the
assistant principal. Yet the assistant principalship is the *beginning* of
a career socialization process. Principals and superintendents are the
outcome of this process. Educators who take on the assistant principal position are in the process of becoming school administrators. As
they do their daily tasks, chat with fellow administrators, possibly
become protégés of more powerful administrators, attend professional meetings and university classes, and observe "how things are
done around here," they learn what constitutes school administration.
They make choices about whether to adopt the values and behaviors
that predominate in the professional culture of school administration. This choice-making is a critical process that determines who
will become a school leader. At the same time, these individuals are
being evaluated: career gatekeepers observe their choices, values,

actions, attitudes, and affiliations. The assistant principalship is an assessment position through which formal and informal district and professional processes are used to decide who should move into high positions of administration.

Yet few scholars devote attention to assistant principals. The National Association of Secondary School Principals (NASSP) issued a position paper (*Restructuring the Assistant Principal*, 1991a), and a few books are now available. Still, few have noticed the person, the position, and the crucial processes that occur in it. A cursory examination of educational textbook indexes shows that assistant principals get much less mention than athletic programs. The 1992 edition of this book filled that gap, drawing attention to and providing a research base for examining the role. First, it *noticed* the assistant, describing the daily work, the special nature of the position, and its rewards and frustrations. Then, by analyzing the selection and socialization of two assistants, it identified key processes that mold those who become assistants and filter out others. Problems emerged from the research on the assistant's work, position, and role. One chapter described these problems and another presented actual and possible policies, programs, and strategies for creative solutions. Thus the book offered practical insights for the educator plotting career strategy and for the professor, the superintendent, or the state policymaker trying to support excellent school leadership. This new edition has a new subtitle, reflecting a changed emphasis. Thus *The Assistant Principal: Leadership Choices and Challenges,* Second Edition incorporates the new realities of administrator shortage, new licensure and training practices, accountability pressures, and other such stressors. It ends with the exciting possibility of using the assistant position as the launching point for revisioning school leadership.

This book is based on perspectives that arise from administrative theory, career development research, and school administration studies, as well as from current policy trends. It also uses the practical advice of persons invested in various aspects of the public educational endeavor.

We listened to the stories, joys, desires, dilemmas, and regrets of many assistant principals. We demonstrate the need to understand the assistant's role and then show how, by focusing on the assistant, we can uncover problems and identify new solutions for reconceptualizing school leadership. There is no better place to begin than with the assistant principal.

Acknowledgments

S pecial thanks to Dr. Kathleen Brown for her insights on current challenges, and thanks also for the down-to-earth comments from several assistant principals, A. J. Mutillo in North Carolina and Bill Walther and Joene Ames in Arizona. Jane Gorey, Wanda LeGrand, and Melanie Schoffner, too, provided gracious and timely help, and Martin Brody provided computer wizard help as well as enthusiastic moral support. We wish to thank the anonymous reviewers, who provided the push to make this book be immediately useful to practitioners.

Corwin Press gratefully acknowledges the contributions of the following individuals:

Janine Jellander
Assistant Principal
Agoura High School
Agoura Hills, CA

Janice Zuege
Associate Principal
Hortonville Middle School
Hortonville, WI

J'Anne Ellsworth
Associate Professor
College of Education
Northern Arizona University
Flagstaff, AZ

James Davis
Assistant Principal
Bethel Elementary School
Concord, NC

Kay Insley
Assistant Principal
Highland Park Senior
   High School
St. Paul, MN

About the Authors

Catherine Marshall is a professor in the Department of Educational Leadership at the University of North Carolina, Chapel Hill. Once a teacher in Rhode Island, her studies and career moves include doctoral studies at the University of California, Santa Barbara; a postdoctoral fellowship at the University of California, Los Angeles; and faculty positions at the University of Pennsylvania and Vanderbilt University before moving in 1991 to Chapel Hill. The ongoing goal of her teaching and research has been to use an interdisciplinary approach to analyze cultures of schools, state policy systems, and the professional development of adults working in organizations. She has published extensively about the politics of education, qualitative methodology, and women's access to careers as well as about the socialization, language, and values in educational leadership. She is the author of *Reframing Educational Politics for Social Justice*, *Leadership for Social Justice: Making Revolutions in Education*, *Culture and Education Policy in the American States*, *Designing Qualitative Research*, and other books, as well as numerous articles on the administrative career, especially the entrant: the assistant principal.

Richard M. Hooley is Superintendent of the Valley Central Schools in the Hudson Valley of New York. Although his advancement was fairly traditional, he was interested in those who reached high administrative posts by nontraditional routes. In his research on this topic, he noticed that the assistant principal was identified as an often-pivotal position. Having worked as an administrator in the Southeast, the Northeast, and the Southwest, his fascination continues even as the assistant principal role changes over time and in the large and small districts he has worked in across the country. Now that Richard is a superintendent seeking to encourage and develop educational leaders in his district, the topic remains germane and is only more complicated by the declining numbers of educators going into administration and the increasing demands set by state and federal accountability measures. Richard taught high school English after earning his bachelor's degree from Wake Forest University. He also earned a master's degree there in gifted education before attending Teachers College, Columbia University, where he earned a second master's and a doctorate in curriculum and teaching.

CHAPTER ONE

What Is Special About Assistant Principals?

Sometimes, at the end of the day, I really wonder why I took this job. It seems like I only bawl out kids, pick up the jobs my principal dislikes, and tell teachers why they can't do something they're really excited about. But there have been times—like when I found a way to help teachers launch a neat project, like watching our team get to the finals in the debate competition—when I feel happy. Not many people know how much I put into making good things happen, but I know.

—An anonymous, but typical, assistant principal

Speaking about the job of the assistant principal, Bill, an outstanding veteran assistant in a large southwestern school district, wrote recently, ". . . people who know how to deal with people and know how to communicate ideas can learn the job quickly. I see a school administrator just like I see a good classroom teacher. Both have goals, understand his/her resources, take risks, stay focused, and organize and plan for the unplanned."

What do assistant principals do? How important are they to school systems? What motivates them to take such a position, and what qualifies them to do so? These questions are seldom asked and rarely

1

answered. Too often, assistant principals are seen as uninteresting—as separate from instructional leadership in their mock-military discipline role and as people at the bottom rung of the administrative career ladder.

One current assistant principal from Arizona says, "We must be magicians and be able to have many skills . . . honed particularly to our site" (Ames, 2004). Another emphasizes the need to be intuitive, and that "you have to multitask and prioritize; if you can't, you won't make it" (Walther, 2004). Thus the position of assistant principal is tremendously challenging, requiring quickness and creativity.

Historically, assistant principals were a phenomenon of secondary schools at the turn of the century, born of the need to manage increasingly larger enrollments in consolidated schools. Mertz and McNeely (1999) write that the position grew out of need and expediency rather than clear and thoughtful planning. To this day, the ambiguity and the random nature of school need or perception of need seem to direct the evolution of the assistant more than any clear data or research.

But the assistant principalship holds a critical position in education organizations for several reasons. First, it is a *frequent entry-level position for administrative careers*. A majority of assistant principals expect to move upward in administration. For this reason, assistant principalships often provide opportunities for observing and interacting with supervisors and learning the behaviors necessary for professional advancement. Second, assistant principals *maintain the norms and rules of the school culture*. They are usually the first ones to handle the most difficult disciplinary problems. Social issues such as poverty, racism, and family disruption help define the world in which assistant principals find themselves.

Directly related to patrolling hallways and monitoring students and their needs, assistant principals must *frequently play the role of mediator*, addressing the conflicts that emerge among teachers, students, and the community. Often it is the demands of federal, state, and local school policies that assistant principals must regulate. Mediation occurs for the sake of maintaining an environment of calm and order; without proper attention to this area, chaos can easily arise. Here lies a great disconnect between training and reality. Assistant principals are not taught how to achieve order in an institutional setting. Instead, they are taught curriculum, leadership skills, best instructional practices, and school law.

Finally, assistant principals *encounter daily the fundamental dilemmas of school systems*. They talk with teenagers trying to stay in school while pregnant, with parents angry that their child must be bused to achieve desegregation, and with teachers who resent and resist being monitored. They fill in when there are not enough qualified substitutes and the English as a Second Language teacher is ill. Their day is a microcosm representing the array of issues that arise when children bring society inside the schools' walls. As a result, they have developed into a prime group of individuals who could, if asked, generate a unique picture of the existing condition of public education.

UNANSWERED QUESTIONS AND CONTINUING DILEMMAS

I once heard a high school assistant principal characterize his position as "the guy who goes up and down the corridors pushing kids back into classrooms." In fact, no one really understands the complexities, lack of satisfaction, and dilemmas within the role of the assistant principal. This chapter identifies those dilemmas—the problems with no simple answers. It tackles the questions raised by our typical assistant principal, questions like these: "What exactly is my job?" "Who knows or cares about what I do?" "How can I find fulfillment in this work?" "Was I supposed to learn in grad school how to plan a pep rally, create a snow schedule, or analyze student test scores?"

Few researchers have paid attention to the assistant principalship. Those studies that have dealt with the topic reveal several intriguing facts. For example, on the surface, there are no substantial differences among the roles of the assistant principal in junior or senior high schools in urban, suburban, or rural schools. Important differences, however, emerge below the surface. Old research reveals challenges that need updates. Gaertner's (1980) study found that while 44 percent of elementary assistant principals are women, women are less likely to obtain secondary school assistant principalships. Croft and Morton (1977) revealed that women are less likely to obtain assistant principalships in a rural or small town than in an urban setting. These facts raise questions: How are the secondary and elementary positions different? Why are some assistant principalships "off limits" to most women?

In spite of the history of the assistant in American public schools, we rely too much on stereotypes and anecdotes. Many questions still remain unexplored by researchers and policymakers. Little attention has been granted to the training and selection, job satisfaction, and motivation of assistant principals. Moreover, few studies have helped the assistant principal focus on the ever-changing, ever-demanding functions of the position. An important unanswered question remains: As assistant principals deal with numerous duties during the course of a single day, how do they derive meaning and purpose from their work?

Attempts to describe the work and its frustrations inform much of the meager research on the assistant principal (Black, 2002; Glanz, 1994; Browne-Ferrigno, 2003; Hausman, et al., 2001). Indeed, one of the more recent books on the subject, *New Voices in the Field: The Work Lives of First-Year Assistant Principals* (Hartzell, 1995), focuses almost exclusively on interviews with new secondary assistant principals on themes such as the pace of the job, student discipline, relationships, and perspectives. The firsthand accounts provide a rich understanding, but it is difficult to find real data on how the job is wrought in most schools and districts. In fact, it has been impossible to find national data on the job or even recent data on the demographics of assistants across the country.

Focusing on the assistant principalship means looking at the administrative training, school culture, job roles, responsibilities, policies and structures of the organization, and daily challenges afforded this specific position. By noticing the interplay of these important elements, concerned teachers, administrators, parents, community members, and taxpayers can begin to understand the nature of the assistant principalship and its intrinsic value to the educational process.

By taking a look at what assistant principals do, we can begin to identify the special nature, the functions served, and the inherent dilemmas in their job. Assistant principals do many of the same tasks as principals. They spend a majority of their time dealing with issues of school management, student activities and services, community relations, personnel, and curriculum and instruction. However, they lack the position, power, and status of the principal. Often the principal delineates their specific tasks and responsibilities. Also, they negotiate with fellow assistant principals on-site. Since the evaluation of assistant principals is often informal or unstructured, their daily performance is analyzed and watched as "higher-ups" decide whether to sponsor or promote them. Knowing they are being assessed as they work in their volatile and fast-paced world is especially stressful. Moreover, the increasingly difficult issue of recruitment and retention of good junior administrators may be tied closely to this stress. A task force in California (the Association of California Administrators) looking at shortages came to just this conclusion.

WHAT DO ASSISTANT PRINCIPALS DO?
THE NATURE OF THE TASKS AND ROLES

Although specific job descriptions vary, most assistant principal positions have tasks in common. Assistant principals handle conferences with parents and students, which may be formal appointments to discuss problems and create a plan to help a student improve or short impromptu responses to a crisis. A second major duty is handling behavior problems, ranging from a long-term strategy for monitoring to a quick reaction to violations. Third, assistant principals work on the master schedule, the "roster" registration, and student attendance as they plan for the smooth flow of people and events. Fourth, they counsel and guide students informally for their educational programs and vocations, basing their advice on information gleaned from constantly monitoring the activities, behavior, and performance of individuals.

Assistant principals also take on public relations tasks as a natural offshoot of working with parents and student activities. Some—not all—assistant principals take an interest in improving curriculum and teaching. With increased emphasis on monitoring and improving teachers, assistant principals are now expected to assist with a major portion of classroom observation.

An old survey documented assistant principals' tasks (Pellicer, et al., 1988), showing student discipline, evaluation of teachers, and student attendance at the top of their list. Since a similar study that was conducted in 1965, duties for graduation, instructional methods, staff inservice, and teacher motivation and incentives had been added by 1985. A recent survey, with 1,230 Texas secondary assistant principals responding, serves as an update (Armstrong, 2004). The changes since that 1985 study emanate from school restructuring and high-stakes testing, which complicate administrative duties.

Interestingly, this study revealed that 37 percent of these assistant principals rotated their duties annually. Although 67 percent

Table 1.1   Duties of Secondary Principals in Texas

Duties Reported in Order, From Most Frequently Reported, to Least

Discipline

Campus Building/Safety

Student Activities

Building Maintenance

Teacher Evaluations

Attend ARD, 504 Meetings

Textbooks

Duty Schedule

Tutorial Programs/At-risk Programs

New Teachers/Mentor Program

Assessment Data/TAKS

Staff Development

Supervise Departments

Community Activities

Attendance

PEIMS

Graduation

Campus Decision-making Team

Lockers

Master Schedule

Curriculum Development

Transportation

Keys

Parking

SOURCE: Armstrong (2004, p. 66).

were satisfied with their jobs, their levels of satisfaction were lower in schools with higher student mobility. Presumably, challenges with attendance, student records, and discipline increase on campuses with high student mobility.

Generally, their tasks require assistant principals to work closely with their principals. They often coordinate with another assistant principal. Frequently, they substitute for the principal. Thus they must work well on a team, be flexible, make quick decisions, and anticipate needs and problems (Austin & Brown, 1970).

Personal and professional disputes, value conflicts, and differing styles and philosophies can be disastrous in such tight quarters; the assistant most often adopts or adapts to the style and philosophy of the principal. Furthermore, assistants are seldom expected to assert leadership by creating new projects or initiatives. Risk-taking must be limited; assistants must confine themselves to supportive tasks, leaving visible leadership to the principal.

Role Ambiguity

The assistant principal seldom has a consistent, well-defined job description, delineation of duties, or way of measuring outcomes from accomplishment of tasks. Along with fixed, assigned tasks, assistant principals pick up multiple jobs every hour. In one study, Mertz (2005) showed that principals assigned tasks in an ad hoc manner, so the assistants speculated they were assigned according to "who did he see first after learning about the task" (p. 18).

Role ambiguity means that the assistant principal's roles and duties include many "gray areas"—ill-defined, inconsistent, and at times incoherent responsibilities, roles, and resources. For example, assistant principals' responsibilities may not include employing substitutes but may include handling the problems that ensue when substitutes are not screened. Some assistants easily develop an understanding of administrative responsibilities and assertively take charge of certain tasks, regardless of their formal role expectations. However, *some* assistant principals may experience a lack of job satisfaction, emotional problems, a sense of futility or ineffectiveness, and a lack of confidence caused by role ambiguity, particularly when the information provided about the job and the actual daily job requirements seem very different (Austin & Brown, 1970; Fulton, 1987; Kahn, et al., 1964; Kelly, 1987; Norton & Kriekard, 1987). Although these problems are well documented, there are no recent studies to review.

Role Conflict and Overload

With so many tasks to perform, assistant principals find that their roles are at cross-purposes with each other. For example, an assistant principal might be required to help teachers develop coordinated curricula, which is a "teacher support" function. But this function conflicts with the monitoring, supervising, and evaluating functions. The assistant may work with a teacher as a colleague in one meeting, and perhaps one hour later, the same assistant may chastise the same teacher for noncompliance with the district's new homework policy. When they must monitor teachers' compliance, assistants have difficulty maintaining equal collegial and professional relationships with them. Also, assistant principals often serve as intermediaries between teachers and students and as the main line of communication to the principal—the person in the middle between constituents and participants in schools.

Assistant principals experience role conflict when the immediate demands of the school interfere with doing the work they value as an expression of their professionalism. Constant monitoring of student discipline, for instance, may require so much time that assistant principals must forsake creative programming in curricular innovation, proactive discipline management, or using their special expertise. If assistant principals are expected to do everything the principal cannot get to, they will not have time to take initiative or focus on special projects.

Finally, assistant principals experience role conflict and overload when it is not possible to perform adequately in all of their assigned roles. This situation is exacerbated when roles and duties are ambiguous, never measured, and never-ending. An assistant principal who is expected to "respond to the needs of community groups" never knows which activities to focus on, how many meetings to attend, or which groups to meet with in order to perform adequately in this role.

Many assistant principals feel overloaded when they try to do well in all assigned duties *and* make contributions by devising special projects. They also may run the risk that the special project is neither noticed nor credited to them when they are evaluated or reviewed. Consequently, such extra work is a gamble at best. There seems to be no end to the ever-evolving expectations and no time taken to say "Well done!" They become discouraged and give up when their principals do not follow through, even after agreeing to support the assistant principal's most innovative ideas (Mertz, 2005).

Role conflict and overload occur when job responsibilities demand so much time, energy, and emotion that little is left for the assistant principal's personal life or professional development. Many assistant principals give up on advanced education and sacrifice time with friends and family as they try to meet the constant demands of their school. As a result, they may become angry, confused, and depressed. They are suffering from the dilemmas of role conflict and overload.

Job Satisfaction and "Dissatisfaction"

Assistant principals who are rewarded for their efforts (by the organization, by the profession, or by their own sense of what is important) should have a sense of job satisfaction. However, some research shows that assistant principals are dissatisfied in their positions. A study of secondary assistant principals in 1996 revealed that they were only marginally satisfied with their jobs and they were not as interested in advancing their careers as they had been in prior studies (Waskiewicz, 1999), but relationships with supervisors and the chance to make good use of one's skills increased job satisfaction. More recently, a survey of secondary assistant principals in Texas found that they were generally satisfied with their jobs (Armstrong, 2004). Older studies provide nuanced findings. The 1970 Austin and Brown study found that many felt they were given low-satisfaction duties such as monitoring discipline and attendance. Furthermore, their multitude of job tasks rarely allowed them to "see a thing through" to its completion (Austin & Brown, 1970, p. 79). The study showed that administrators believe that most of the assistant principals' assignments do not give them a high level of discretionary action. Their work is constrained by rules and understandings about their "place" and limits on their range of initiative.

A study in urban Houston and town and rural areas of Kansas (Croft & Morton, 1977) found that assistant principals felt higher satisfaction with duties requiring expertise and administrative ability than with those requiring clerical ability. The study also showed assistant principals as having higher satisfaction than Austin and Brown (1970) reported. Nonetheless, assistant principals deal with the dilemma of deriving satisfaction from this risky and sometimes powerless position. They have a great deal of responsibility but little discretion, and they are under constant scrutiny. As they seek satisfiers, they respond to pushes and pulls from their specific school site, their sense from previous professional experience about what is important, and the school system's rewards and incentives.

Much can be learned about job satisfaction by examining why people leave the assistant principalship. Austin and Brown found that assistant principals left for better salaries and higher status. A significant number left seeking greater professional challenges, including greater involvement in the school's educational program and a desire to innovate. One would conclude that they seldom find these satisfactions in the assistantship. Calabrese and Adams (1987) found that assistant principals had a greater sense of powerlessness and alienation than did principals. Those with advanced degrees, especially the doctorate, had much higher perceptions of alienation and powerlessness. Again, these problematic findings in old research provide insights for needed new research.

Career Incentives

Probably the most powerful reward and incentive for most assistant principals lies in the possibility of using the position as a stepping-stone to administrative careers, particularly for line positions (as opposed to staff specialist positions). The assistant principal may perform the same tasks as principals (concerning budget, facilities, student affairs, curriculum and instruction, and public relations), which prepare them for moving up in the hierarchy.

In school administrative careers, a common career route to the superintendency is that of teacher, secondary curriculum specialist, secondary assistant principal, secondary principal, associate superintendent, then superintendent. The elementary principalship appears to be a dead-end position, while the secondary principalship provides opportunities for districtwide links (Carlson, 1972; Gaertner, 1980; Gallant, 1980; Ortiz, 1982). Thus there exists a real possibility that good performance as an assistant principal will directly lead to the next administrative line position, the beginning of the march up the career ladder. According to norms of the profession, career success in administration is measured by the attainment of higher power, status, pay, and a higher administrative position in the hierarchy.

Many view the assistant principalship as a step up the career ladder. Few practicing administrators prefer to remain in the assistant principalship; the Austin and Brown study showed that between 40 and 50 percent of all assistant principals advance to other professional posts. A minority (39 percent urban, 29 percent suburban) of the respondents expected to make the assistant principalship a lifetime career when they entered the field, while a majority expected to be promoted within their own districts. This situation creates role dilemmas from which two questions emerge:

1. What is the level of effort exerted by assistant principals who perceive themselves as simply "passing through"?

2. What happens to assistant principals who realize they have plateaued at the assistant principal position?

It is important to examine whether the assistant principalship has intrinsic rewards or incentives for those who will not move up.

Moving into the assistant principalship is considered (by many educators and in terms of pay scales) to be a promotion, a reward, and a signal that one has potential for leadership. However, some assistant principal tasks are menial and routine, possess low visibility, lack evaluation and review, and provide no opportunity for creativity. Without opportunities to take risks or attempt risky projects, these individuals have no opportunity for special recognition and reward in those leadership areas. Clearly, being the disciplinarian will not provide the assistant principal with visibility or allow interaction with people in higher administrative positions.

However, some assistant principal tasks, assignments, or activities do offer opportunities for exposure to superiors, provide for frequent reviews, allow for expansion of knowledge and exercise of discretion, and allow involvement in special risky projects; they allow and encourage assistant principals to innovate and receive credit and feedback that enhances job satisfaction and opportunity for advancement. Typically, these tasks are on the boundary between the school and the community or other units of the school system (e.g., task forces managing state policy, the PTA, or district computer committees). Interestingly, these opportunities to distinguish oneself and obtain recognition from district administrators almost always involve interactions with adults, not children. When assistants develop interpersonal skills with community people, superiors, and other adults, they can learn skills for career mobility. Assistant principals who assume such tasks are more likely to get the attention and sponsorship of superiors and the motivation to move into higher positions. Thus there is built-in temptation for assistants to concentrate their efforts in areas that facilitate upward mobility rather than in areas focusing on the immediate needs of the programs and people in their own school.

Assistant principals who have little opportunity to move into higher positions (because of their tasks, low turnover in administrative positions, or district restrictions) are plateaued, facing the possibility of ending their careers in the assistant principalship. They are left to find rewards and incentives within their current position. In Chapter 3, we present new research on the satisfactions, adjustments, and delights found by "career assistant principals."

Thus we see that the position can be shaped to be quite rewarding. Still, while they perform important tasks, assistants seldom are rewarded adequately. Often their tasks are conflicting. While schools cry out for leadership and creative efforts for reform, assistant principals' opportunities for initiative are constrained. This presents problems but also policy opportunities. Professional associations and policymakers seeking ways to support new leadership will do well to address these dilemmas for assistant principals.

POLICY CONCERNS IN THE ASSISTANT PRINCIPAL ROLE

Policymakers do not pay attention to the assistant principal. They do not sponsor studies or even collect data on this position. As a result, they miss rich opportunities to make a difference.

Recruiting and Retaining Leaders

Policymakers and administrators, especially superintendents and personnel directors, desperately work to recruit and retain entry-level teachers. However, the challenges of recruiting and retaining good school leaders, including assistant principals, begin with the challenge to recruit educators generally.

The recruitment and retention issues for assistant principals are usually ignored because people focus on teachers and principals. Although these are, truly, interrelated careers and positions, policymakers too quickly leap past the assistant position in their deliberations. In a 1998 survey of superintendents asking about their difficulties in recruiting principals, they reported that candidates were most discouraged for the following reasons:

- Compensation was insufficient compared to responsibilities
- The job is generally too stressful, and

- The job requires too much time.
- Other reasons—concerning parents, community, societal problems, accountability pressures, bad press, funding for schools, and no tenure—were far less worrisome for candidates (Educational Research Service, 1998). Although this survey focused on principals, it may shed light on assistant principal recruitment. These issues, however, may have shifted by now as a result of increased accountability pressures from the No Child Left Behind Act (NCLB).

Identifying Appropriate Training and Selection Systems

Assistant principals are usually selected because of their visibility and success as teachers, department heads, counselors, or administrative interns. Likewise, the administrative candidates who conform to work requirements and advance tradition are most likely to be selected for promotion. But in the process, many talented, innovative educational leaders are rejected for entry-level administrative positions. Many others with potential for creative educational leadership may look at the assistant principal position and decide not to enter administration. The need for good training and selection guidelines is a pressing policy issue.

State policymakers, professional associations, and university professors ponder and debate the formal training and experience required for administrative positions. We are still trying to develop a set of understandings for the field of educational administration and describe the appropriate skills and functions that are necessary.

Formal course work does not transform people into good educational leaders. Furthermore, there exist very few specific, agreed-upon, definable criteria for selecting administrators. Efforts (e.g., the National Association of Secondary School Principals [NASSP] Assessment Centers and Interstate Leadership Licensure Consortium [ISLLC]) at training and evaluation actually weed out some with innovative approaches or may rely on assumptions that no longer apply. The reforms and the pressing challenges of the standards-based education movement in the new century require reexamination of assumptions about educational administration. Since the assistant principalship is an entry-level position and often the first formal administrative position that a person holds, previous administrative experience would be an inappropriate prerequisite. No evaluation instruments have been devised specifically for measuring the ability of the assistant principal. Tests would be difficult to devise because the assistant principal's tasks are so varied across schools, districts, and regions. Therefore university programs, state certification requirements, staff development, selection systems, and professional association meetings and publications are often designed with only a best-guess effort to address the requirements of the assistant principalship.

Encouraging Innovators

School systems need vigorous imaginative leadership to meet the challenges presented by community change, declining resources, state and federal accountability, and national concern about the quality of education. Numerous studies have raised the question of whether educational leaders have the ability or the desire to be creative in addressing schooling problems. Indeed, the stated purpose for charter schools is to create a place for innovation and new ways of framing education by releasing such schools and their administrators from the burdensome requirements of state and federal government.

The selection system for administration typically weeds out people with divergent ideas. Often, teachers have a conservative bias (Lortie, 1975). Therefore, assistant principals and other administrators are selected from a pool of rather conservative people. To start with, the more creative, imaginative, reform-minded, and innovative people have already been filtered out. Then the selection and training process continues this filtering by discouraging those with innovative, divergent, and creative ideas.

In the process of training and selecting individuals, organizations teach a person to "make decisions by himself, as the organization would like him to decide" (March & Simon, 1958, p. 169). They are socialized to think and work within the status quo. People who raise questions and challenge the system are more likely to be viewed as misfits than as potential leaders. People who have conflicting feelings about administration, school programs, and incumbent administrators, and who challenge existing practice, will be less likely to be seen as trustworthy and loyal enough to be included in the administrative group.

People who are different (either because of different backgrounds or ideas or because they are minorities or women) take special risks when they separate from teachers and attempt to become administrators. They risk becoming the "marginal man" (Merton, 1960), who neither fits with teachers nor is included with administrators. Diversity in the first years of the twenty-first century is defined more broadly than ever before, and all of these differences fall outside the very conservative administrative mold. Examples of exclusionary characteristics beyond gender and race might include economic, philosophic, political, and intellectual diversity as well as sexual orientation and the fact that a candidate's spouse is from a different racial background. Therefore people who *are* selected as administrators are likely to be those who are similar to previous administrators, people whose ways of thinking and acting coincide with tradition.

Because of litigation and liability issues, the nature of administrative work these days is conservative. The tendency of school administrators to make safe decisions, avoid risk, and make short-term plans for measurable programs prohibits innovation. Thompson (1967) explains these tendencies by pointing out that administrators have incomplete knowledge of cause-and-effect relationships. Furthermore, he notes that "organizations can thwart the exercise of discretion by establishing inappropriate assessment criteria as bases for rewards and penalties" (Thompson, 1967, p. 120). People who have ambiguous positions, who are evaluated by vague or inappropriate criteria, are very dependent on others' judgment. They risk losing power and rewards when they exercise discretion or independent judgment. So there is an administrative bias in favor of certainty, a bias in favor of quantifiable results, and a reliance on precedent rather than innovation. Intolerance for ambiguity and favoring quantifiable measures of cost-efficiency rather than wide-ranging discussions of social goals are natural reactions to administrators' need to maintain control over the organizational environment.

Another factor that stifles innovation is the depth of knowledge a new assistant principal must have to be effective. From the point of view of a superintendent or principal, it is critical that the assistant principal support the established routines and guide teachers in the established procedures. Clearly, assistant principals spend most of the early years in their role learning procedures and the school culture. One very large forward-looking school district in the Southwest created an exciting new administrator academy, in which new administrators log hours with central office department heads, learning about process and procedures. This setup guarantees that the district's desire for a smoothly run system will prevail, perhaps stifling innovation. The academy, then, becomes a training school.

Administrators, when overloaded by work demands and worried that they will be judged on efficiency rather than on creative leadership, will make safe decisions, avoiding ventures (e.g., in democratic leadership or community involvement) that tend to decrease their control and increase their risk. They will bend to political pressure when they are uncertain about the best stance to take in a conflict. They will put their energies into programs that will be understood, assessed accurately, and rewarded. They are unlikely to search for creative or long-term ways to address dilemmas in schooling. And the assistants who observe the selection processes (for entry into these and higher positions) will learn that risk-taking and divergent thinking can hurt their careers. Interestingly, much of the professional development and literature prepared for superintendents is focused on risk-taking!

Thus a pressing policy question remains: What recruitment, selection, reward, and assessment system will ensure that schools hire and train innovators, leaders of reform, builders of school-community integration, and participatory managers?

Encouraging Instructional Leaders

Still another pressing question for those who train and select educational leaders concerns how we can identify, encourage, support, select, and reward administrators who care about the instructional program. These concerns stem not only from educators' general orientation and interest in the quality of curriculum and instruction but also from the body of research indicating that effective schools have, among other things, people who take leadership in curriculum and instructional programming. On the other hand, some reform efforts aim to empower teachers—the educators most closely attuned to classroom and curricular concerns—to have more decision-making power, discretion, and responsibility for instructional leadership. But can and do site-level administrators (assistants or principals) "lead" instruction?

Who owns the "instructional leadership job," and how is it coordinated? Analyses of the daily activities of principals and assistant principals show that their time is taken up with personnel, school management, and student activities and behavior, although they claim to value instructional leadership and program development functions (Gorton & McIntyre, 1978; Greenfield, 1985a, 1985b; Hess, 1985; Kelly, 1987). With the tightening of accountability for students' academic performance, no site-level administrator can duck instructional leadership work. Assistant principals and principals can, however, empower the teachers, facilitate the decisions, and help devise strategic improvement and continuous improvement plans. No initiative or reform will occur without grassroots support from teachers, and the administrator has a big hand in moving that forward.

Thus, under current traditions and structures, the assistant can be an instructional leader only in rare instances or in more nuanced ways. Furthermore, in leaving teaching to enter the administrative ranks, assistant principals may lose credibility in instructional matters (Greenfield, 1985b; Little, 1984; Spady, 1985).

The effective schools literature indicates that maintaining safe and orderly environments, building wide awareness, and committing to high levels of student progress are part of instructional leadership. But being an assistant principal may actually undermine educators' ability and affinity for instructional leadership if they advance to higher administrative positions. Quite possibly, the duties of assistant principals prevent them from developing as instructional leaders. Often their tasks take them away from classrooms and curriculum and place them in roles of managing rather than working with teachers. One must ask: Do teachers, assistant principals, and principals with the training, ability, and affinity for instructional leadership actually receive career rewards and promotions?

Observation of assistant principals (Marshall, 1985a; Reed & Himmler, 1985) raises doubts that their tasks and roles allow them to develop competencies in curriculum leadership and teacher supervision. The center of their daily activity is maintaining organizational stability. Policymakers must pay attention to the assistant principalship in their debates and directives aimed at locating and supporting instructional leadership.

Providing Equal Opportunity

As a key position for entry into administration, the assistant principalship is an important focus for policy concerns about equal opportunity. Assuring access to administrative positions for women and minorities is a matter of equity as well as a matter of providing role models for students, of expanding the definition of competent leadership, and of maximizing the use of a pool of talented personnel.

Women and minorities have not attained administrative positions as often as men, even during the 1970s and 1980s when affirmative action policies were established. Women are more likely to be in staff positions (consultants or supervisors of instruction) than in the assistant principal and principal positions that are direct lines to the superintendency. The norms enforcing compulsory heterosexuality in school administration are so embedded that the profession seems quite incapable of even talking about gay and lesbian school leaders (Blount, 2003; Marshall & Ward, 2004). Presumably, some persons with disabilities would be winnowed out by explicitly stated job specifications about heavy lifting and intervening in fights.

It is useful to identify historical trends. Several studies of minority representation in administration indicate that minority administrators often lost their jobs or were demoted during school consolidations in response to desegregation mandates and/or economic constraints (Coursen, 1975, 1989). For example, in Florida's consolidation movement in the 1960s, nonminority principals often retained their positions or advanced while minority principals were demoted to assistant principalships or to special projects administration, with limited power, or were placed back in the classroom (Abney, 1978). Affirmative action policies have not compensated for these losses. Ortiz (1982) also found a general pattern of minorities being placed in administrative positions to supervise minorities and special projects, positions that were neither at the center of power and decision-making nor on the career path toward higher positions.

It appears that the assistant principalship is a good career stepping-stone for men but not for women. Gaertner (1980), in her analysis of administrative career patterns, found that women are less likely to attain the positions (particularly secondary assistant principalships and principalships) that lead directly to the highest administrative positions. Furthermore, female teachers are more likely to be in elementary schools, where assistant principals are few and far between. Prolman's (1982) study of principals found that among those who had prior administrative experience, men were far more likely to have held an assistant principalship. In her sample, only one woman had held an assistant principalship prior to her principalship. Most women had held positions in the central office as directors of programs or as supervisors. More recently, of principals surveyed in 1994, 54 percent had been assistant principals or "program directors" prior to their principalship and 27 percent had been athletic coaches. This pattern has held steady over the years, although it is a less pronounced pattern in private schools than public (Fiore, 1997). Policymakers need to examine recruitment to the assistant principalship to see how it can be altered to promote equity in administration. We need better national statistics on the trends in hiring women and minorities as assistant principals (more on this in Chapter 4).

As the twenty-first century unfolds, policymakers are still seeing these trends and making only weak interventions. Policies generally are race-neutral and gender-neutral, at best, and the issue is framed as if it would be merely about opening up opportunity. Recent changes in licensure pay little to no attention to the historical pattern of women's and minorities' unequal representation in administration or the informal socialization processes that recruit and support white males.

Few districts, universities, foundations, or policies provide incentives, scholarships, or special support for women or minorities. As revealed in a survey about recruiting principals, superintendents said that minority recruitment was an issue for 35 percent of districts overall and for 67 percent of urban districts. However, superintendents said they had plentiful qualified female applicants. Thus, for policymakers unconcerned about equity, the "minority problem" is worse than the "women problem."

To achieve equitable support and access for women *and* minorities, the informal recruitment and support processes must be changed so the professional culture of school administration is more enticing and supportive. Currently, it takes too much perseverance and defiance of norms and expectations for women and minorities to take on the extra stresses that all school leaders face. In her study of female teachers with leadership potential, Wynn (2003) found that they just could not see anything appealing about administration, especially when it required giving up attention to instructional matters and distancing themselves from children, including their own! Thus policies cannot work with mere statements about equal opportunity.

As a result, much leadership talent is systematically cast to the wind, leading to a crisis in numbers and a talent drain. Policymakers can reverse this pattern: "Instead of waiting for individuals to self-select administration, educational leaders must be identified and groomed in a systematic way that facilitates the recruitment of potential leaders among women and minorities" (Crow, Mecklowitz, & Weekes, 1992).

Empowerment and Participatory Management

Principals have considerable autonomy not only in assigning tasks to assistant principals but also in defining the style of the working relationship between the principal and the assistant principal. Old research found that assistant principals had few tasks that allowed problem-solving and discretionary action, concluding with the belief that "a do-as-you-are-told policy in assigning duties to members of an administrative team is a very short-sighted one as measured by the well-being of the school" (Austin & Brown, 1970). They found that "principals more frequently than assistant principals believe that assistant principals are invested with a substantial measure of responsibility for important functions of the school that require the exercise of good judgment" (p. 47). These findings reflect a tendency to keep assistant principals in a subordinate position within a specific chain of command, a hierarchy with the principal controlling the work of the assistant principal. Recent research (Mertz, 2005) and anecdotal evidence indicate that this has not changed. Such a view seems inappropriate for an organization in which the workers are fellow professionals. Emphasis on hierarchical control can subvert efforts to work cooperatively toward common goals. District policymakers should be concerned about the professional development of aspiring educational leaders and should direct attention to the assistant principalship.

Participatory management strategies include incorporating lower-level management in decision-making so that their concerns and ideas will be heard. Administrators who have a part in making policy are more likely to implement the policy in their school sites (Berman & McLaughlin, 1978), and communication and cooperation are enhanced. In addition, such participation gives administrators a sense of satisfaction and belonging (Gorton, 1987; Shockley & Smith, 1981).

When principals see the assistant principal only as someone to do the undesirable tasks, they lose the opportunity to multiply administrative efficacy. Such a "mop-up" assistant principal merely supplements the work of the principal. However, principals who work as administrative teams with their assistants could *multiply*, not just supplement, their effectiveness. Such an administrative team approach is more than the sum of its parts. School district policy-makers need to identify structures for supporting administrative teamwork at the school site.

To establish a climate for participatory management at the school level, districts and principals can, and sometimes do, create the structures and attitudes that facilitate participation. In addition, principals need to recognize their responsibility to provide their professional colleagues with opportunities for satisfying work, adequate support, advanced training, and effective resources. Principals who view the assistant principal as the person who does everything that the principal dislikes undermine the possibility for administrative teamwork. On the other hand, principals who learn a more collegial and less hierarchical style of leadership will get the best from their fellow professional educators—assistant principals, teachers, specialists, and other support staff.

Collaborative leadership is the essence of site-based management. Administrators should lead and facilitate this site-based management. This means that when facing a question such as "How will we address our declining reading scores?", the administrator can and should present the data and facilitate brainstorming as well as the implementation plan.

Unfortunately, NCLB has erased the initiatives of site-based management in many ways. There still may be ways that this new accountability facing schools from state and federal governments can lead to opportunities for collegial leadership. For example, a rising need for good data collection and analysis now exists in schools as never before. An assistant principal might take up that task and provide information for decision-making efforts. Similarly, when data are collected and analyzed, a broad-based plan for using the data to improve instruction and achievement is needed. Facilitating a committee to implement the results seen in the data leads to collaborative work, not only by the administrative team but also in the wider school community. Strategic plans offer this same kind of chance to lead an implementation effort based on the test or achievement data. The division of tasks also can drive a more collaborative culture. When the principal, for example, is partially responsible for discipline or tracking attendance along with the assistant principals, some of the hierarchy is erased. A principal working alongside assistant principals in the trenches, so to speak, creates an environment of shared decision-making and problem-solving.

The Plateaued Assistant

A majority of assistant principals view their position as a necessary career step to higher positions. However, when upward mobility is not possible, what happens to these people? Many assistant principals must face the reality that they will end their careers in the same position. Many entered administration late in their work lives. Some are seen as particularly valuable in the position and hence will not be moved. Others are labeled as potentially troublesome if promoted; still others are viewed as "not fitting in." And in districts with declining enrollment, there are simply no viable opportunities for advancement. Assistant principals frequently face such realities with a sense of failure and frustrated aspiration. Yet these realities continue to confront educators as they sense their careers reaching a plateau and the possibility of upward movement becomes more and more remote.

The frustration of the plateaued assistant principal is exacerbated by the assumption that success means upward mobility. The hierarchy, status, and reward system in education supports that assumption.

The frustration is intensified when the assistant principal is required to spend long hours doing unpleasant tasks that have no clear, measurable outcomes. Under these conditions, the assistant principal has little power or opportunity to redefine tasks or plan for better management. Both the long hours and the sometimes-limited mobility are serious frustrations, but they fade in significance in states where teachers are relatively well paid because of a long history of strong union activity. In the Northeast, where this is often the case, assistant principals could actually make less than the teachers they are supervising or give up substantial stipends that teachers receive for coaching and other extra duties. The new assistant principal could actually lose salary when he or she accepts this entry-level administrative post.

Recent research and policy concerns about the administrator shortage *should* highlight the plateaued, dissatisfied assistant principal. It would make sense to pay special attention to those who are feeling unappreciated or underpaid, needing a wider vision, and/or underperforming. Rather than lose those underachievers, special supports could transform them into high-capacity leaders.

Can the assistant principalship be defined in such a way that it is seen as a valued and desirable position? Are there policies and structures that would enable people who feel no pressure, obligation, or desire to move into a higher position to find fulfillment and continuous challenge as "career assistant principals"? This is a concern for educators and policymakers.

RECENT REALIZATIONS AND DEVELOPMENTS AFFECTING THE ASSISTANT

Schools have always had to find ways to work with changing demographics. Patterns of immigration, migration, and homelessness have always presented challenges to school leaders. But leaders realize the need to do more than simply provide access. They are not always prepared to embrace not only cultural diversity but also single-parent families, families in poverty, and families in which all the adults work full-time with no extended family to watch over kids. Similarly, it is not enough for school leaders to simply increase the use of crisis intervention teams to deal with problem kids or special education laws and regulations. Furthermore, the risks of hasty decision-making are accentuated in this increasingly litigious society and with the likelihood of more children falling through the cracks.

Now, NCLB requires more and more academic interventions, before and after school as well as during the day. But the assistant principal is challenged to meet this mandate when parents cannot transport the kids there or when a parent does not have enough influence to compel the child to attend. What should the assistant do, when not solving these matters means the school is out of compliance?

Assistant principals must be very careful, given the increasing disillusionment of parents and kids with the expectation that doing well in school will earn the student a good job. Some students and their parents simply do not buy the old messages about "good school performance getting you to the good life."

Finally, assistant principals find themselves acting in *loco parentis*. They have to cope with an immediate crisis when they must act, daily, in spite of the increasing ambiguity and tension over the role of schools in mediating kids' identities and values regarding issues such as sexuality, religion, drugs, students' sense of self, and their self-presentation. The assistant principal may feel silly deciding that the kid with the scanty tank top or low-rider jeans must go home. The assistant principal might know that providing a condom would be the very best way to help the boy in front of him, but it would be illegal.

Much can and should be done to pay attention to assistant principals who, like Mr. Black below, struggle daily in helping schools function.

Bruce Black's Assistant Principal's Diary

Now that he has retired after eight years as a high school assistant principal, during which he wore out the soles of two pairs of shoes every year, Black (2002) shared parts of his diary from his first year on the job:

September, first day: I walk the halls' bathrooms, three lunch duties. The noise during eighth grade lunch is like a playoff game in a domed stadium. I am not sure how many miles I put in but I was in bed by 8 p.m.

End of September: . . . the principal is dealing with the kid who came to Homecoming dressed as a condom while I am dealing with the parents who want compensation for their child's broken glasses.

October 1: Student with a serious eating disorder . . .

October 7: Janitors see me about a student who defecated on the floor—secretaries laugh about me and the Mad Crapper.

October 11: Must remove a student—a big guy from the special ed room. I'm only 5'7" but I'm fast.

November 29: The hockey player I suspended for chewing tobacco says he'll sue me.

December 3: Today I was physically assaulted by a kid who thought I was to blame that he's been truant and thus suspended.

December 4: There's a stolen snowmobile in my office.

February 3: A student I saw during the day attempts suicide that night. She is okay now . . . I am lucky; I work with a great group of counselors.

February 9: A bomb goes off in the cafeteria—student made it, following instructions on the Internet.

> March 7: My daughter phones and tells me about a phone message that says "I want to kill you and your family."
>
> Mr. Black recalls managing the unpredictability of his job with a sense of humor. He actually enjoyed the challenges of the position, but after eight years, he said, "juggling too many things at once eventually wears you down" (p. 38). His twenty-nine years as a middle school principal seemed relaxing in comparison with his assistant principal years (Black, 2002).

SUMMARY

A close analysis of the daily work of assistant principals provides a picture of their important functions at the school site. However, the analysis also reveals unanswered questions and opportunities for improvement through policy. By focusing on the assistant, policymakers could affect instructional leadership, innovation, and equity for women and minorities as well as recreate the position to be more than just a career stepping-stone. In paying special attention to assistant principals' training and recruitment, policymakers could affect the supply and quality of future educational leadership. Most assistants would welcome such attention.

One is left wondering if the assistant principalship isn't, as currently construed, a rather poor orientation to creative leadership, even though it is the usual stepping-stone and training ground for higher leadership positions. Chapters 2 and 3 provide deeper descriptions of current practice. Then, in the last chapters of this book, we note promising trends, programs, and policies and propose new ways of structuring and conceptualizing leadership.

DISCUSSION QUESTIONS AND ACTIVITIES

1. As a practitioner, why do you believe policymakers, the media, and universities do not pay more attention to the quandaries and challenges of assistant principals?

2. You may have noticed exceptions (including in your own experience) to the statements made in this chapter (e.g., you may know people who are secure and happy as assistant

principals or school districts where many women and minorities hold the position). How can you explain these exceptions?

3. Conduct a library search on your own, or as a group, to identify the kinds of issues raised about assistant principals.

4. Make a list of questions and conduct phone or e-mail interviews with several districts' personnel directors and/or with several professors of educational administration to identify the kinds of issues they raise about assistant principals. This might be of use in contract negotiations for assistant principals.

5. Ask several successful principals and superintendents to discuss their fondest and worst memories about their years as assistant principals.

6. In your district, how often do assistant principals meet to discuss their roles and district initiatives, and with whom do they meet?

7. What opportunities exist or can be imagined, for you as an assistant principal, to become involved in a high-profile project for your school or district as you balance the other duties of your job?

8. What could be done to limit the time you and other assistant principals spend on discipline?

9. What curriculum or data projects could you assist with or facilitate at your site?

10. As an assistant principal, what issues do you feel were missed in this chapter to fully articulate the challenges you have experienced?

CHAPTER TWO

How Do Assistant Principals Get Their Jobs?

To analyze the process by which assistant principals learn their roles and build skills, we look at two case histories of assistant principals, which illustrate some very common elements in assistant principals' learning and in the processes for attaining these positions. We use the cases to identify the issues in training and selection and possible alterations for improvement. The cases are simulated, but they are based on three decades of informal observation, on reviews of literature, and on analysis of administrative careers.

THE CASE OF TIM GEORGE

Tim George's skills just "grew like Topsy." He never attended any staff development or university courses that taught him how to carry out his daily tasks except for a workshop about creative discipline. He had always read articles about innovative curriculum that were published by his professional association, but generally he had not learned assistant principal skills from any courses or reading. In his frank, just-between-you-and-me moments, Tim denounced the education courses in his master's degree program. He once said, "You wouldn't believe one prof; he showed slides of his trip to Chile so he could justify his tax deduction! I never really grasped the statistics in the class on testing and measurement, but I got a B+ anyway. I did get a better picture of what kids are going through in the courses on human development, but I never could figure out how to fit that into anything like managing crowds of them at a basketball game."

Tim admitted, however, that he often selected courses based on their convenient time or their reputation as "gut courses" and that his choice of programs was confined by his desire to get the master's degree and administrative credential cheaply at the closest college. When asked about this 10 years after he graduated, he acknowledged that "college course work can give an overall picture, but each school and district does things differently . . . it's all about learning the system you are in and then adapting your skills and knowledge."

So, then, how did Tim George acquire the skills and knowledge that enable him to perform as an assistant principal? "It's real difficult to tell," he admits. "I think it all came from just *doing* things and watching other people do things. When I was a teacher I knew a lot about what the principal was doing because I was one of those rovers, without my classroom. The principal asked me to help with early-morning crises like substitutes and late buses. I saw how he managed staff and parents, how he kept things under control. I learned a lot from watching him. I guess the best breakthrough came after the time I complimented him on how he cooled out two mothers who were upset about our sex education program. He explained to me how he assessed the situation and figured he had better be very careful to calm their fears but still uphold district policy. From that time on he'd tell me stories about how he handled things. I learned a lot from him."

Many of his life experiences, even from childhood, provided Tim with training that helped him be an effective assistant principal. He felt that playing basketball in high school, working in a grocery store during college, having the support and understanding of his wife (who tolerated his long working hours and did not complain when their "extra luxury money" paid his tuition as he worked for his administrator's certificate), and coaching the Little League team (which included two school board members' children) helped him in his position.

During his four years as a teacher, Tim George dealt with the usual problems of controlling classes, getting along with other teachers, and feeling that nobody appreciated the difficulties of his job. Over time, he began to feel that teaching and managing a classroom were not challenging enough; he wanted to do something different. Tim also was learning a great deal about teamwork, school spirit, school-community relations, and basic crowd control as the coach of the junior high basketball team.

While Tim was a teacher, his superintendent asked him to serve on several district committees: one on equalizing coaches' pay and implementing Title IX and one for coordinating the social studies curriculum so that students would have an appropriate and sequential curriculum from elementary to senior high. Working on these committees gave Tim the opportunity to talk with principals and teachers from other schools. He enjoyed representing his school, helping to define the issues, gathering information, and making presentations to small groups. Tim's principal called on him more frequently, asking him to oversee the afterschool recreation activities, prepare reports for the superintendent, and even work during the summer on planning schedules for the next year. Every time the principal left the building, he appointed Tim to aid the assistant principal.

Tim was especially proud of his master's project: he convinced his own and another junior high principal to let him implement, for one semester, a behavior modification approach on their "top 10 most incorrigible problem kids." That semester was an exhausting one for Tim. In addition to the project, he had to manage his regular classes and troubleshoot in two schools. He devised measures and demonstrated successful results in his project, and district administrators applauded when he presented the results at one of their meetings.

Tim was probably the first person to know that the current assistant principal wanted to move out of the assistant principalship. He was not surprised when the central office sent a notice advertising the job opening to each school, to the local university, and to the state administrator association. The notice stated:

Immediate opening: Junior High Assistant Principal

Particular duties: To be arranged

Qualifications: Experience with some administrative duties; master's degree and administrator certification required

Salary: Negotiable, as per contract, and based on prior experience

Apply by January 12

Tim knew that at least eight people applied. The selection committee consisted of the principal, the guidance counselor, and the president of the PTA.

Although he initially felt confident, Tim became nervous during the selection process. *He* knew that the principal depended on him, but he was not sure how well the principal knew that. He knew that the PTA loved him, and he had served them well; but the guidance counselor might push for some unknown person who had several degrees. The competition included Eleanor Bowen (voted outstanding teacher in the high school) and Bo Tomlinson (high school social studies teacher, winning football coach, and boyhood friend of the school board president). He knew about them only through gossip; all the other applicants were just worrisome mysteries.

During his interview, Tim spent more time trying to figure out what the committee wanted to hear rather than thinking out his answers. First they asked about the courses he had taken; then they asked him his views on school-community relations. He struggled when they asked why he wanted the position and what he expected to be doing in five years. The interview was upsetting. He knew that he had stiff competition. Also, the committee did not give him a chance to talk about the things he had done. Instead, it was as if they were more interested in his opinions and his ability to spew out some line off the top of his head without offending anyone. He left the interview in despair, knowing that the others, coming from other schools, would be able to look good by talking about their accomplishments.

The next day, the principal offered Tim the job. He complimented Tim on his contributions to the school and expressed pleasure and relief that Tim would immediately take over assistant principal tasks. They had some limited negotiations over salary and discussed the process of getting school board approval. One school board member was harping on instructional leadership and had clearly wanted Eleanor Bowen. There were also questions about Tim's age and the fact that he had not taken many certification courses. The school board agreed that Tim could complete course work within a year. Finally, the selection committee asserted that their process had come up with the best candidate. There was unanimous approval, and Tim was on the job before the week ended.

The principal told Tim later, in confidence, that the selection committee was able to weed out many applicants just by phoning principals, a few college professors, and a few other trusted educators. Some applicants were described as troublemakers, difficult, uppity, and grandiose planners. Others were eliminated because they hadn't taken many courses for advanced degrees or certification. Some were eliminated just because they "looked fishy." For example, why would a woman from out of state be applying unless she was having trouble in her current position? Or why would a man who had his doctorate and had already been an elementary principal in a small district want an assistant principalship? After these applicants were weeded out, Tim still looked the best. Of the three finalists, he could most easily take over the tasks of the job, and there would be no need for the principal to teach him the goals, problems, constraints, and routines. The principal praised Tim's performance in the interview, saying that he showed energy, willingness, and a good attitude.

It was natural that, on being appointed junior high assistant principal, Tim would be assigned the task of disciplinarian. He says that he learned by doing the job, but he had some rude awakenings:

> The first week on the job I tried to work on the plans for integrating the social studies curriculum. When they hired me they were really impressed with my work on that committee, but now my time was eaten up by patrolling halls, cooling down students who were acting out! My behavior modification approach didn't work after awhile; most of the kids got wise to it. Then I had another shock—the time we had parents demonstrating outside our school, demanding "the truth" about the amount of asbestos in the school. We didn't have any answers, the superintendent had been avoiding the issue, and the press was hot on it. The principal was away at a meeting so I was really put on the spot, totally unprepared. Well, I somehow muddled through, but the kicker was that I found out that my principal had *planned* to be away, knowing these demonstrators were coming! I was really upset, but I was forced to realize that it was *my* job to do anything the principal couldn't or didn't want to do, and I'd better not complain about it. He said we were a team, and it was clear that we had to present a united front to teachers, students, parents, and the superintendent. Once I told him I wanted some of my time set aside for implementing the social studies curriculum and for analyzing the other areas of instruction, but he seemed angry instead of impressed, telling me to put more time into handling unruly kids. He did, however, use my ideas, and we are now working toward curriculum improvement.

Tim described many instances in which he somehow learned what was acceptable practice by noting his principal's reactions or by making his own informal assessments of results.

By his fourth year on the job, Tim George was known throughout the district as a tough but effective assistant principal, and he was eager to move up. His principal would be retiring in three years, so Tim suspected that he probably could walk into a principalship, if he could be patient. But his disciplinarian tasks were getting to him. He really wanted a chance to try out some of his ideas on personnel motivation and curriculum. With one more course, he would finish his master's degree in administration and pass the state and university tests for principal certification. Tim felt that he had demonstrated his skills in the assistant principalship, but he also knew that, as currently construed, the assistant principalship was too limited a position for him. For his own satisfaction, he would have to find a new position soon.

THE CASE OF ALICIA BROWN

Alicia Brown had taught for 12 years. She loved teaching high school kids but felt a restless need for change. When her curriculum innovations failed to allay the restlessness, she took on such tasks as student association sponsor and chairperson of the school board's committee on student-teacher-administrator relations. At that point, Alicia's principal and several district-level administrators urged her to begin course work for administrator certification. Although she knew she could do the job, the idea of leaving teaching and the comfort and camaraderie she shared with teachers, who were mostly women, to hang out with administrators, who were mostly men, was less than enticing. Still, it seemed an opportune time because her two sons were in college, and she noticed that neighboring districts were promoting quite a few women. She had sensed, long ago, that it would be frowned upon if she tried to be an assistant principal while her boys were younger. She had heard about the "bad old days" when job interviews might include questions about her plans for having children or even about birth control. She knew such probing was now illegal, although young women still said they felt they had to offer reassurances in job interviews. Now, her husband, who was absorbed in his own career, was pleased that Alicia was so encouraged and excited about her own work, even if the job seemed designed for young people willing to work 60-hour weeks.

The university course work was stimulating; it helped Alicia attach names to things she had observed in schools. Courses on organizational behavior, school law, community relations, curriculum, and school finance helped her place daily school events and concerns in perspective. She found herself less upset about confrontations with parents; instead of raging about cost-cutting in the school budget, she began to realize the importance of selling education to the taxpayers. Alicia was especially fascinated by her organizational behavior course discussions revolving around workers' motivation and reward systems, and she enjoyed writing a paper applying the theory to teachers and students. The university program required Alicia to complete an internship, which she designed so she could work with both a school and a district administrator. This provided her with a variety of settings in which to sharpen her skills and to create and implement several projects that gave her visibility and credibility among administrators. Alicia completed her administrator certification program and most of the course work for her doctorate.

Unfortunately, Alicia's district was suffering from declining enrollment, and the only job openings were in special education. She had applied for five positions, all in neighboring districts, although her university adviser sent her details of positions all across the state. She interviewed for an elementary principalship and an assistant principalship, but in each case the districts chose someone from their own district. Some of the job descriptions seemed to designate a preference for a man or a bodybuilder, when the list of requirements actually stated that applicants must be able to lift 100 pounds.

Alicia's principal, a staunch supporter of hers, moved to a distant superintendency. She missed his encouragement and advice but kept in touch by e-mail. She kept alive the image of herself as an administrator by joining the new women administrators' network and volunteering for myriad tasks that would keep her hand in administration.

After four years of applying for posts, Alicia attained her first real administrative position as assistant principal in the junior high located in her own district. During the selection process, Alicia learned that her competitors were all men younger than 32, with considerably less university training, expertise, and experience in curriculum and instruction (which had been stressed in the job announcement). She knew the job was hers, given her qualifications. In addition, the school board was embarrassed that they had not hired any female administrators in the last eight years.

Alicia's story continues with her on-the-job learning and her pride in the projects she initiated for afterschool activities. But she was shocked and disillusioned when her schemes for staff development and revitalizing the curriculum were put on the back burner in favor of discipline tasks. After only five years, she was coming to a gradual realization that she must find another position; she constantly wanted to challenge her principal and make changes but could not.

The break from this no-win situation came when Alicia received a fellowship along with her application for a doctoral program in reading. Although reading was not directly relevant to her assistant principal work, she had always been interested in it, and working at the middle school had only underscored her concerns about reading deficits in the district. Alicia once again threw herself into university course work (while continuing, albeit with reduced commitment, her role as assistant principal); she earned her doctorate and a position in the central office as director of reading. Because she was 55 years old, she envisioned finishing her career in this position.

How Assistant Principals Learn About the Role

Tim George's and Alicia Brown's histories are similar to the role learning, selection, and career steps of many assistant principals. They show how people select themselves or are recruited and how perception shapes the thinking of candidates. These case studies illustrate that the school site's needs affect selection, and they show how the formal selection typically proceeds. In this section, we ferret out the common elements in how assistant principals are motivated for administration, attain an assistant principalship, are selected and trained, and learn to fill their positions.

Career Decision-Making

As people make career choices, they feel pushes and pulls that come from (a) the picture they have of the desirability of the career, (b) the likelihood that they can possess the required qualifications, and (c) the degree of support they will have for taking the risk and making the extra effort. Generally, they try to figure out whether they can fit comfortably in the career.

Educators assessing the desirability of the administrative career observe the tasks, functions, status, satisfactions, and stresses of those in the roles. As Tim and Alicia observed assistant principals, their observations had different meanings for each. While the tasks and the people doing them were already very familiar to Tim, this was not so for Alicia. Most were males with backgrounds more similar to Tim's (e.g., short teaching career, experience in sports). Indeed, this linear male experience has been described in research focused on gender equity (Edwards, 1993), retention of administrators (Hooley, 1997), and tracking careers in administration (Shakeshaft, 1987).

Personal and family considerations affect career decision-making. Educators who observe the long hours, the heavy responsibility, and the strain on the family life of administrators may say, "No way, not for me!" Some conclude that the job demands too much personal sacrifice, that the financial and personal costs are too high for traveling to night classes for certification and advanced degrees, with no scholarships or district support for sabbaticals. Some have spouses who will resent the time away from family. Many, especially women, decide that these personal costs are too high when there are no role models for them and, indeed, there are career norms that support white males but present barriers to others.

Thus Tim's and Alicia's progression to the point of aspiring to administrative careers was a process of interaction between their own characteristics and the signals from the career environment. The positive signals were strong for Tim, but it was less obvious to Alicia that she would fit comfortably in administration. For her, the supports were less tangible, and her entry into the career was delayed.

Anticipating the Roles

People who are appointed to assistant principalships have already gone through "anticipatory socialization," a period in which they think about administration; watch administrators' activities, behaviors, and attitudes; and start to transform themselves into administrators. During this period, they separate themselves from other teachers and find ways to demonstrate their abilities, favorable attitudes toward administration, and desire to become part of the administrator group. In this way, they attract the attention of superiors who may encourage, mentor, and support them, even becoming their sponsors. Aspirants have usually observed administrators intensely long before they take on any administrative duties. They have found visible ways (e.g., Tim's coaching, Alicia's course taking, and the district committee work of both) to try out the roles.

Role Model Learning

Assistant principals need more than a job description and abstract knowledge of administrative duties and skills; they need to see how the particular tasks are carried out by effective practitioners. Assistant principals seek role models whose style in managing situations, students, parents, and superiors seems to be practical and functional. In many cases, assistant principals use several people as role models, acquiring the effective behaviors that best fit their own situations, abilities, and personalities. Frequently, role models become mentors when they take time to explain the ways things are done. Then the aspiring administrator has a tutor as well as a model for learning the skills and roles of an administrator.

Tim's principal served as his role model, mentor, and sponsor. After Tim demonstrated interest and respect, his principal opened up with stories about how schools work. In her early teaching years Alicia had no clear role models; it was hard for her to imagine that administrators could be female. Now her male principal was supportive, but there was no bond of mutual identification. Her university classes were full of aspiring women, however, and she received encouragement and ideas from them.

Task Learning

Perhaps the strongest learning experiences for assistant principals come when they take on, or are assigned, certain tasks. Teachers may be asked to form committees, to develop criterion-referenced tests, or to coordinate curricula. Department heads have the task of developing a budget for materials; assistant principals may be assigned the task of coordinating afterschool activities. No amount of abstract training or reading substitutes for the intense learning that occurs as a person takes charge of a task.

Task learning forces a person to learn skills and attitudes (e.g., teamwork and risk-taking) and gain knowledge of specific needs.

At the same time, it provides an opportunity to visualize oneself performing new tasks and then demonstrate to others one's effectiveness. Thus the teacher or assistant principal who takes on the responsibility of a particular task (whether it is the faculty duty roster, the science fair, the intramural program, the task force on testing, or even patrolling the lavatories) has an opportunity to learn, self-assess, and attract the attention of superiors.

When task learning is guided by a mentor, the aspiring administrator will benefit from feedback, assistance, and support. Task learning may be facilitated by courses, workshops, and internships that include opportunities for reading, discussing, and reflecting on the theory, research, and practice of administration and leadership.

In many cases, informal task learning is easier for people whose backgrounds are similar to those of other administrators. Then mentoring and sponsorship are facilitated by a sort of natural empathy and the desire of administrators to work with someone very much like themselves. Sponsors naturally choose to help people who have similar family, religious, social class and social clubs, gender, and race characteristics and backgrounds. Valverde (1974) has called this the built-in replication formula in sponsorship.

One solution to the absence of mentors or sponsors in school administration is supportive colleagues. Teacher colleagues who have an interest in administration decide to enroll in graduate school together. As they share in the process, they develop a support system and a de facto discussion group. After class or while carpooling, they talk about the schools where they teach. These aspiring administrators work on group projects together for class and may end up as administrative colleagues at different schools in the district. These experiences provide them with valuable professional connections and networks, even as they discuss opportunities and openings in the search for administrative posts.

PROFESSIONAL SOCIALIZATION: THE MIX OF FORMAL AND INFORMAL TRAINING

In most professions, aspirants must go through prescribed formal university training that provides the theory and skills for a sound knowledge base. For administrative certification, they must seek the official sanction of the state. The gatekeepers of the profession must ensure that aspirants exhibit the appropriate attitudes and meet the appropriate ethical standards. However, in the new administrator's world, these efforts may be entirely disconnected. Universities offer few if any courses on ethics and professional standards of behavior, and there is no course on the daily work of discipline, although most assistant principals would report that it consumes much of their work life. In education, like many other professions, the training can be intensive and rigorous, requiring a great deal of time, sacrifice, and isolation from the real world. As a result, many people are weeded out.

An assistant principal in Arizona recently reflected, "Think about how the whole thought process starts. Some know early on that they want administration. But many are minding their own business teaching and are approached by an administrator, making suggestions. Some are groomed from the beginning by districts that pick who they think are the best and brightest. When superintendents are teaching admin courses they pick and groom individuals . . . " (J. Ames, personal communication, September 20, 2004).

The formal training in educational administration is typically less than systematic. Usually, aspiring administrators take courses in their spare time as they continue with their full-time jobs and family responsibilities. There is considerable debate over whether educational administration is really a distinct profession with its own knowledge base, theory, and ethical standards. Politicians and state bureaucrats exercise tremendous control over the training, selection, and monitoring of educational administration professionals. They, more than educators, decide on the knowledge base and skills for the profession, which may account for some of the disconnects between training and practice.

Assistant principals encounter formal training structures: state certification requirements direct aspiring administrators to take courses and show evidence of professional development. These aspirants have passed teacher certification requirements and frequently have worked toward master's and even doctoral degrees. Pay and tax incentives and some state laws induce educators to continue course work in universities. Therefore a great deal of formal training for aspiring administrators comes from university courses taught by professors who usually have limited experience as practitioners.

State departments of education, state boards, and special commissions usually determine the general goals of administrator certification, guided by the advice and involvement of professors and professional educators' groups such as the NASSP, the University

Council for Educational Administration, the American Association of School Administrators, and others. (Chapter 4 identifies trends in certification.) States vary in the degree to which they update and monitor the implementation of these goals in certification programs. They also vary in whether or not people must earn administrative certification before taking an assistant principalship. Waivers are frequently granted when a school district wants to hire an individual who is still earning the credential.

Aspiring administrators may acquire information and training through professional association conferences, workshops, district staff development programs, and state programs such as "executive academies" or "professional development seminars." However, once the candidate becomes an assistant, it is difficult to participate in professional development opportunities since he or she is such a critical player in the daily life of the school.

Aspiration Building and Self-Selection

Adults form and modify their aspirations for careers as they gather feedback from families, peers, and significant others such as professors and superiors. Teachers considering administrative positions search for signals of support and encouragement and take action to show their worth long before they ever actually apply for an administrative position—a sort of aspiration-building and self-selection process. When the signals are positive, they raise their aspirations and start to devise ways to move from their current positions to new positions that are more central, powerful, and responsible and higher in status and pay. Sometimes they feel a "tap on the shoulder" (literally or figuratively) when some knowledgeable and potentially powerful person makes an extra effort to help them discover their leadership potential. With encouragement, they take risks, associate with new people, burn bridges, estrange themselves from old affiliations, make sacrifices for extra training, and show their worth. They often find ways to "try on" the roles and tasks, taking on quasi-administrative tasks, sometimes as volunteers, and getting the attention of superiors. They watch current administrators with a new focus, as if trying to see themselves in those roles. During this self-selection phase, they notice that administration is not always fun; that there's a "teacher versus administrator" phenomenon and a chilly reception in the teachers' lounge; that administrators must see things more globally; that administrators have little control of their time, leading to the phenomenon of "administrator burnout"; and that administrators have a kind of "emotional Teflon" (Sigford, 2005).

The Formal Selection Process

People who work in organizations can sense a kind of career map, a charting of the paths to follow and the kind of person to become in order to attain certain positions on that career map. They observe who does and does not get rewarded, and they see the steps that others have taken to get to desired positions. Such information is seldom charted as a formal career map, but the information becomes folk knowledge—known by everyone, unstated law, a part of the assumptive worlds.

The formal, stated administrative selection process does not delineate such informal maps and folk knowledge. Instead, districts advertise position notices listing the functions of the job, the deadline for applications, and minimum and/or desired qualifications. Often the qualifications listed are (a) previous administrative or leadership experience, (b) university course work or degrees, and (c) state certificates.

A look at 2004 assistant principal job descriptions from states including New York, Massachusetts, Florida, Kentucky, Wisconsin, Arizona, and California reveals these commonalities:

- Reports to the principal and main task is to assist the principal;
- Supervises and evaluates instructional and support staff;
- Assists with field trips, testing, data gathering on student performance, the school improvement plan, administering employee contracts, public relations, inservice programs and teachers' professional development, physical plant, budget, student attendance, discipline, guidance, substitutes, technology, curriculum, extracurricular activities, and more;
- Keeps the principal informed, stays involved in own professional development, uses appropriate interpersonal skills, sets high standards for self and others, etc., etc., etc.

Some list multiple duties and required skills and then add, "Additional duties are performed by the individuals currently holding this position and additional duties may be assigned" (Browning Public

Schools, 1999). The notices usually specify qualifications including master's degrees, certification, and three or more years in teaching. Sometimes they indicate a possibility of hiring someone who is still learning certain skills, as when they require "willingness to learn budgetary and supervisory responsibilities" (Sarasota County School District, 2001). Sometimes they specify physical demands, as in "while performing the duties of this job, the employee is regularly required to walk, sit, and talk or hear . . . The employee must occasionally lift and/or move up to 100 pounds. Must occasionally be able to restrain students . . . to run after students . . . deal with students and adults in tense and confrontational situations . . . " (Killeen, 2001).

Thus the challenge of the position is right there, in writing, for those who wish to go into school administration through this tough entry point. The position is full of responsibility—yet with the main task of being an assistant.

States, usually in cooperation with universities and professional associations, establish criteria for attaining certification for positions in schools. Thus part of the formal structure of selection for administrative positions is earning the degrees and certification expected and demonstrating, through degrees, courses, and job experience, the stated requirements for positions.

References, tests, and interviews. The formal part of the selection process may include a request for references from universities and practitioners. Most applicants ask for letters from supportive colleagues, community leaders, former bosses, and respected professors. A letter from a high school coach saying that Tim is a good guy may be important for offsetting rumors of a bad temper. Similarly, a letter from his professor detailing Tim's intellectual progress in his curriculum planning course can make a difference. Letters are part of the formal process, but the informal process—phone calls and casual conversation among administrators who are in touch with the selection process—is more important than letters.

Applicants are given little information about how the selection process will proceed. In some districts (especially urban ones), routine personnel office procedures are spelled out, well known, and followed. More often, applicants depend on tidbits of information from friends who have some access to the selection committee to find out the procedures, the expectations, the dynamics among the people who control the process, the top candidates, and the timing of the process.

Infrequently, school districts use simulations and testing to assess candidates' skills and values; more often, skills, experience, and values are assessed by a formal interview process, which sometimes includes bringing in school and community representatives to serve on selection committees. Usually the school's principal has a great deal of influence in selecting the assistant. NASSP Assessment Centers, where administrative candidates' skills are evaluated as they work on activities, are, in some districts, applied to the assessment of assistant principals. (Chapter 4 provides details about assessment centers.) A great deal of research and action has centered on ways to improve the selection process of principals and superintendents, but less attention has been paid to assistant principal selection.

In many cases, assistant principal recruitment and selection is left to the site principal, with a formal selection process in place to lend legitimacy. In most cases, assistantships are filled by applicants from inside the district. Assistant principalships are posted within the district, although some districts advertise in statewide professional association newsletters. One seldom sees national advertising for the assistant principalship. However, as the administrative job market continues to tighten, publications such as *Education Week* and other state and national advertising and posting sites (including electronic postings) now include assistant principal vacancies. In fact, principal vacancies are now being filled with the help of search consultants, complete with district brochures that were once reserved for superintendent searches.

The Informal Assessment Process

The administrator grapevine—conversations, asides, gossip, phone calls within and among districts—serves a key information and referral function in selection, especially in large districts where hiring decisions are more ambiguous or diffuse. Incumbent administrators hold common assumptions about the attitudes, backgrounds, and skills of aspiring administrators. They share their assessments of candidates through this grapevine, which is probably the most powerful selection structure in the school system. Freed from the fear of legal reprisals that often result from putting words on paper, administrators gossip. Their observations, combined with their values and biases, are used by selection committees as they select the top candidate. This is the "good old boys' network."

The selection committee makes decisions quickly, as soon as a satisfactory choice is available. Decision-makers in organizations often conduct a limited search for information, choosing the first acceptable solution. There is, therefore, a preference for insiders—previously socialized and tested individuals. This may be especially true in filling unanticipated assistant principalship vacancies. In a school lacking an assistant principal, crucial daily order and maintenance functions are neglected.

Informal assessments may include indicators of candidates' loyalty, personal background, helpfulness, intelligence, initiative, willingness to perform essential tasks to maintain the rules and order, and professional knowledge. These are all informal criteria for inclusion in the administrator group. These assessments—coupled with the particular selectors' preference for certain skills and certain types of task learning as well as experience to meet the current needs of the specific school—are often critical deciding factors in administrator selection.

Informal assessment probably helped Tim George. For example, school board members, having seen him work with children, may have made favorable remarks about him when inquiring about the selection process. Such remarks could quiet any protest about his slow progress to certification.

In many instances, candidates are labeled "poor on interpersonal relations" on the basis of informal assessments. A phone conversation about Alicia Brown's strong stance in the Title IX implementation committee could lead to such labeling. On the other hand, her university professors could have brought attention to Alicia's intellectual abilities if the professors were connected in any way with the network. In larger districts and more historically unionized areas such as the Northeast, administrative unions can help to articulate a hiring process for their membership and for aspirants. Clearly, such pressures could advance or diminish the informal processes depending on the relationship of the union with the superintendent and board.

Ambiguous and Negotiated Expectations

The assistant principalship consists of poorly defined tasks, ambiguous expectations, and few formal measures for evaluating achievement or task accomplishment. It is difficult to know how to predict, measure, and select people with high potential for success in the position. Therefore people may be selected on the basis of informal references, "gut feelings," or perceptions that they will "fit in" and fill whatever needs arise.

Candidates whose opinions and attitudes are congruent with the selectors, who have had opportunities to visibly demonstrate their willingness to pitch in and their loyalty to the particular school site and/or district, will have more success in this situation. Such candidates may be able to negotiate with selectors if they do not meet particular formal requirements. A candidate who has no administrator certification may convince selectors that quasi-administrative experience will suffice as long as the certificate is earned in the near future. Or a candidate may convince selectors to view Little League coaching as equivalent to a requirement for "experience in coordinating and developing curriculum."

RECENT TRENDS AFFECTING RECRUITMENT INTO THE POSITION

District personnel and state policymakers realize that the crisis in recruiting and retaining teachers, as well as concerns about diversity, present new challenges for entry into school administration careers.

Crisis Recruitment

Public policymakers pay considerable attention to the shortage of qualified teachers, the looming shortage of principals, and the turnover of highly visible superintendents struggling to manage urban schools' challenges. To forget or neglect the assistant principal is a huge mistake.

A large proportion of education administrators are expected to retire during the next 10 years. In addition, increasing enrollments of school-age children will also have an impact on the demand for education administrators. The U.S. Department of Education projects enrollment of elementary and secondary school students to grow between 5 and 7 percent during the next decade (see www.college grad.com). Not only are existing principals retiring, but fewer individuals with credentials are applying, so the crisis intensifies when administrative applicants are few or lack experience. As a result, districts may recruit in crisis or emergency mode. In the absence of an adequate pool of applicants, districts may fast-track educators who may not want to make the transition to administration or who need more training before taking on the huge responsibilities of the assistant principal position.

Enrollments are expected to increase the fastest in the West and South, where the population is growing, and to decline or remain stable in the Northeast and Midwest. School administrators are in greater demand in rural and urban areas, but pay is generally lower there than in the suburbs. But the stress, the accountability requirements, and increasing governmental regulations discourage teachers from taking positions in administration. The increase in pay is often not high enough to entice people into the field.

Early Exiting

The trend in teachers leaving their jobs has its parallel in school leadership. Except for the superintendency, assistant principals have, arguably, the most unmanageable stress and unanswerable demands. Their stresses and demands are less visible than the principal's, but assistants, especially as novices, are less experienced at developing coping strategies. Moreover, as the frontline administrator, they often face the greatest level of confrontation from students, parents, and teachers. By the time a difficult individual meets with the principal or the assistant superintendent, the positional authority of the higher office calms the parent, student, or staff member. Principals and central office staff may never hear the screaming, accusations, and cursing that take place in the assistant principal's office.

Balancing "The Look" in School Sites

The percentage of female and minority principals is increasing nationally, so one assumes that this is true for assistant principals as well. However, the numbers do not meet the needs for one emerging trend. Districts and schools increasingly try to include at least one female and one minority administrator. While this is never overtly stated in recruitment materials, savvy educators know it is a reality. Thus white males may not bother to apply when they know the school's current administrative team is all white males, and women or minorities may not apply when they know a site already has "the look"—that is, the "politically correct" balance of gender and race among administrators, given the school's population. Unfortunately, as districts work to create a more diverse administrative office in schools, perceptions take over. Society is so sensitive to affirmative action that when a minority or a woman is hired, the assumption is that race and gender were primary considerations. Likewise, perceptions drive applicants. Although candidates may or may not apply based on the racial or gender balance at the school with the vacancy, districts and human resources departments understand that basing a search on such demographic factors is discriminatory and could lead to lawsuits.

SUMMARY

The two case histories and the analysis demonstrate how personal life circumstances, informal interactions in the community, school district activities and needs, staff development, special projects, and special professional interests interact with formal course work, certification processes, and district policies for selection and hiring. In this interactive process, assistant principals like Tim and Alicia are tapped on the shoulder. They get support, mentoring, access, and the requisite training to go through the formal steps to attain an assistant principalship. One can see, too, that differences in this interactive process will affect one's orientation to the role of assistant principal. Different degrees of support, access, task learning, university experience, and personal life situations affect a person's ease of entry and degree of satisfaction. These, in turn, affect a person's ability to use the assistant principalship as a stepping-stone to a line or staff position in administration.

Clearly, the way assistant principals are trained and selected has important implications for who becomes an assistant principal. It determines what sort of orientation an assistant principal has to educational leadership. It determines how assistant principals carry out major functions such as implementing policy, maintaining the school culture, and providing instructional leadership. And it determines whether assistant principals are able to fill the role in a constructive and satisfying way. By focusing on the assistant principal position, policymakers and district personnel could do a great deal to address current crises in school leadership.

The remaining chapters identify and describe new research programs, policies, and structures that affect assistant principals. They offer recommendations and information about possible ways to reconceptualize the assistant principalship and to restructure the role definition, training, selection, and administrative career ladder once we have recognized and focused on the position's importance in the scheme of school administration.

DISCUSSION QUESTIONS AND ACTIVITIES

1. With all the projections of shortages of school administrators, can you find evidence that people are seeking ways to improve the recruitment and selection of assistant principals? Start with your district and your experience. Have you seen any recruitment improvements or changes since you were selected for your position?

2. Construct a game plan for how the prospective assistant principal can attain his or her most-preferred position, including a checklist of actions to take.

3. Think of the two most talented and competent teachers you have known in the past four years. Write a job description that would entice them into an assistant principal job. Obviously teaching and assistant principal positions require different competencies, but after writing the job description, discuss ways to bridge those differences so that more talented educators might take assistant principal jobs.

4. How could these job descriptions be written to entice more women, more people of color, and more people who are most satisfied when working closely with children's learning?

5. Speculate, based on your observations and experience, whether Tim's or Alicia's stories would differ depending on (a) whether their district were urban or rural and on (b) the diversity in the demographics of the students and the other administrators at the school sites: if they were younger, older, persons of color, if either were gay or lesbian, if either had a highly respected spouse or other family member. Cite personal experiences or anecdotes about your school or district related to the hiring of these underrepresented groups.

6. Since white males hold most administrative posts and certainly the most powerful ones, describe how their similar backgrounds might lead to homogeneous leadership. That is, if most of these males come from backgrounds teaching math or social studies and coaching, what is lost by continuing to hire similar individuals?

7. What parts of the case studies did you or your discussion group find inaccurate or false? Which elements did you perceive as accurate and true based on your experiences?

8. Make a list of typical teacher leadership tasks such as department chair, advisor to the drama club, etc., and write a sentence or two arguing how each task translates into administrative preparation (just as we often hear coaches use their experience to support their administrative candidacy).

9. Underpinning much of the discussion in this chapter is "politics"—school, small town, even bureaucratic. Discuss the role that politics plays in your situation and talk about how you and people in your school manage it.

10. As an assistant principal, you care very much about how new colleagues are selected. What suggestions would you give to your district for recruiting and selecting the kind of colleagues you think are needed?

CHAPTER THREE

Progress in Understanding the Assistant Principal's Role

The role of assistant principal is full of numerous and sometimes humorous anecdotes. The undercurrent of adolescent hormones is an often-ignored element in schooling, which research generally ignores but assistant principals see daily. One high school assistant principal recalls having to quash the student-led rumor that he was dating his fellow assistant principal—a rumor generated solely from the day they "did a walk-through in a classroom together." The same assistant principal found himself suspending a boy for possession of pornography, then having to fend off the boy's mother's demand that teachers be asked, "Don't you look at pictures of naked women, too?" Delights abound, too, in honing a newly minted teacher's lesson plans, seeing an increase in diverse parental involvement, even in just having bus duty go smoothly. These are assistant principal realities, as are the spitballs and stink bombs, the assessment of the propriety of students' apparel, and the painful dilemmas emanating from the truly pressing needs of poor families' children. These are not captured in sterile survey research.

Too often, the little research on the assistant principal is done with simple surveys. But surveys of tasks and assessment of job satisfaction do not adequately capture the essence of the assistant principalship. Most of the studies of assistant principals have been normative, surveying tasks, duties, aspirations, status, selection, effectiveness, and perceptions (Black, 1978; Fulton, 1987; Greenfield, 1985a; Lawson, 1970; Norton & Kreikard, 1987; Pitts, 1974; Preston, 1973).

Frequently, these ways of understanding lead to dead ends—to seeing the assistant principal as hatchet man, activity coordinator, handyman, and firefighter (Reed, 1984). Only by being an assistant or at least following them through their days can we gain deeper insight into their roles, functions, feelings, needs, and aspirations. This chapter describes several studies that used a field study or case study approach aimed at uncovering these realities. This is a more fruitful way of understanding the role of the assistant principal (although we still need good trend data on the assistant principal's status and realities). These efforts help researchers examine how assistant principals function in the complex organization called school (Greenfield, 1984).

RESEARCH ON THE WORK AND WORK ARRANGEMENTS

A field study of eight secondary assistant principals in southern California (Reed & Connors, 1982; Reed & Himmler, 1985) investigated the nature of the work and its relationship to the high school as an organization. Twenty-eight hours of observation and interviews provided an in-depth picture. The study showed the assistant principal's functions for stabilizing and transforming schools and showed the ways in which the assistant principal's work is primarily focused on organizational maintenance.

Schools establish stability through structures like the bell schedule, the student handbook, the code of conduct, and the curriculum. The assistant principal facilitates some of this by arranging the master schedule, which regulates curricular activities. Schools also establish stability through the extra-curriculum as it springs from and reflects community values. Assistant principals use the extra-curriculum as a way of maintaining surveillance over students' conformity with community and school values.

Assistant principals' work is facilitated by their acute senses (attuned to the smell of marijuana, for example) and their "referral system" by which teachers, parents, students, and other administrators tell them when organizational stability is threatened. The study showed the importance of the assistant principal in supporting organizational regularity and promoting organizational values. These are particularly important skills in an increasingly chaotic society. The school's stable, predictable environment is enormously important for students whose lives are nothing but chaos once they leave the school campus. This analysis highlights the ways assistants' work supports community values. Assistants' work is primarily with students; part of their work is being highly visible to students. Their workday is unscheduled; they respond immediately to unpredicted events. They control extracurricular activities and use them as a way to enforce community values through student attitudes. Their work also is critical for implementing state expectations (laws and policies) as they translate state requirements (e.g., minimum curriculum) into everyday regularities (student schedules and the master schedule).

While their main "tools" are the positive aspects of schooling (e.g., activities), assistants spend most of their time with the negative aspects of discipline. Consequently, they may become cynical. Even when not directly intervening, they are patrolling. They offer support (e.g., pleasant conversations inquiring about a student's hobby or encouraging a student to run for student body office). They remedy the situation when there are disruptions.

The researchers found that disruptions are classified into several categories. They may be minor, such as a kiss on campus—passing events in which few rules and values are seriously challenged. "Not very serious disruptions" (e.g., tardiness, truancy, inappropriate dress) do disrupt order and are covered by rules. "Serious disruptions" (forgery, defiance of authority, gambling, fighting, threatening a teacher) are covered by rules and are threats to school values. "Very serious disruptions" occur rarely and are not covered by rules. They threaten the school and community values of students and adults. "Streaking" is an example.

It should be noted that the term "very serious disruption" has acquired new meaning in the aftermath of the massacre at Columbine High School and the anxiety of September 11th. A whole new world of responsibility has grown up in recent years, requiring assistant principals to develop comprehensive emergency plans and train in emergency and command management. In many states (such as New York), safety plans are reviewed by the state education departments. Lock-down drills and emergency evacuations are now part of professional development for assistant principals. Bomb threats, sign-in procedures, and violent threats against others or the school are major concerns for administrators at all levels. Threats of all kinds are now taken very seriously and can eat up hours of an assistant principal's time when handled properly. Such threats must also be catalogued and reported to the State Department as part of the NCLB legislation.

Assistants' sanctions range from "extra work" to parent conferences to expulsion recommendations. Assistants see themselves as projecting images ranging from policeman and "mother superior" to "father confessor" and helper. Their decisions about which sanction to use and which image to project depend on (a) the type of disruption, (b) the student's reputation and disciplinary history, (c) the context, and (d) the load on the system. The assistant principal uses rituals that enable misconduct to be addressed and remedied in a way that maintains stability.

This old study, by exploring assistant principal work in the organizational context of the school, identifies the crucial functions performed, not just the tasks, as they relate to overall school functioning. Such studies are needed now to update and enhance our appreciation of the complex work performed by assistant principals. However, an in-depth analysis of the stories of new assistant principals (Hartzell, Williams, & Nelson, 1995) revealed how little new assistant principals understand the nature of their "concealed" jobs. Isolated in their classrooms, few teachers have intensely observed assistant principals. The concealment continues when assistants are ignored in university programs and generally ignored in research.

RESEARCH ON THE SOCIALIZATION OF THE ASSISTANT PRINCIPAL

Another research project (Marshall, 1985a; Gross, 1987; Mitchell, 1987; Scott, 1989), through case studies of 20 assistant principals, examined the organizational processes that affect assistant principals as they are socialized to be effective and comfortable in school administration.

An early analysis (Marshall, 1985a) described the "professional shock" encountered by these entry-level administrators. Their early tasks were to develop the ability and willingness to find the culturally appropriate response to these shocks. Performance in these tasks affected (a) whether they were seen as competent and (b) whether they could be comfortable and remain and/or move up in their administrative careers.

The first task was deciding to leave teachers and teaching behind. This entails tremendous self-analysis, combined with strong signals from the organization indicating that opportunities are available. For example, some were motivated by anger about the status quo, inspired to become a leader to change things; others were groomed and sponsored by incumbent administrators.

The second task was analyzing the selection process not only for their entry but for upward mobility in the career. Each new assistant takes careful note of the qualities, skills, functions, personal characteristics, backgrounds, and styles of the persons selected for the career. Sometimes this yields shocking information. For example, one woman realized that she had remained an assistant under a succession of new principals, in each case teaching the novice principals the ropes. Finally, she was told (after her sponsor retired and affirmative action pressures subsided) that she was seen as the "principal maker." In contrast, another female assistant's analysis of the selection process made her conclude that she projected the right image and was favorably placed for upward mobility as long as she continued exhibiting the right behaviors, attitudes, and image.

Maintaining a calm front in the face of culture shock was the third task. New assistants are shocked at how unprepared they are for the array of tasks they confront. They are surprised to see things that seem unprofessional, unfair, and wrong. One said, "I was shocked at the underhanded things done on the job—manipulation, violation of confidence" (Marshall, 1985a, p. 39). Another was astonished to realize that "they clearly wanted a white man" (p. 39). Yet another was surprised to see strategies devised to solve problems even if the strategies damaged the instructional program. But these assistants had to maintain a calm front in spite of their confusion and stress.

The fourth task was defining relationships with teachers. Taking the administrator's perspective, the new assistant suddenly is supervising and evaluating teachers, who are sometimes friends and former allies. Now, suddenly, the job includes judging and "shaping up" those who are viewed as incompetent or lazy; to do that job, assistants must create a new superordinate-subordinate relationship with teachers.

The fifth task was learning the art of the "street-level bureaucrat." When faced with the need to implement policies and meet pressing needs with chronically scarce resources, street-level bureaucrats learn how to remake policy. They modify goals; ration services; convince students, parents, and teachers that they can wait for services; and "fudge" on reports. When there aren't enough qualified substitutes, they carefully find ways to circumvent procedures so they get the best ones. When a districtwide homework policy must be monitored, assistants learn to use that monitoring to fill more pressing teacher evaluation needs.

The sixth task entailed identifying, demanding, and protecting one's areas of responsibility or "territory." Certain responsibilities (e.g., discipline, duty rosters, handling the older students, parent conferences) become known in the district or the site as critical, visible, and tough assignments. Even with written job descriptions, assistants could lose their territory to a competing assistant or to myriad other new tasks, so they must assert their command over their territory and maintain control.

The last task involved discipline management. Assistants must learn to cope diplomatically with the realities they see. Such realities include (a) teachers having a bad day and taking it out on a kid, (b) the need to "learn the art of bluffing" (Marshall, 1985a, p. 50), (c) the need to individualize discipline (e.g., calming the emotionally disturbed child rather than using forceful discipline), and (d) creating preventive systems (e.g., frequent touring and chats to sense tensions, creating a stable of good substitutes to avoid disruptions).

As they encounter these tasks, assistants are socialized to fit into the administrative culture. They create their own interpretations of policy to fit school needs and develop related political skills for presenting explanations of their school's needs and strengths to parents, teachers, students, and people in high district office positions. The analysis shows new assistant principals defining relationships with teachers in terms of "us versus them"; it evidences the difficulties women have in asserting their territory for managing discipline; and it demonstrates the array of enculturation tasks they encounter—above and beyond the obvious tasks of buses and rosters.

In addition, the research uncovered the coping mechanisms of assistant principals who are plateaued and who are working under principals whom they do not respect. It showed them coping with their own questioning of the very structure of schooling. It showed them making choices between molding themselves to fit the administrative culture and advance within it or considering whether to defy the culture or even leave the profession.

More intensive analysis of the same research led to the delineation of assistant principals' assumptive worlds (see Marshall & Mitchell, 1991) and the typology of orientation to the career (Marshall, Mitchell, & Gross, 1994).

CONSTRAINTS ON BEHAVIOR
AND VALUES: ASSUMPTIVE WORLDS

Using the same case studies of assistants but a new perspective of micropolitics, Marshall and Mitchell (1991) identified the "assumptive worlds" of assistant principals. These unstated rules are understandings about limits on their roles and their expression of values. A fledgling administrator might be forgiven initial naiveté, but continuously ignoring those assumptive worlds would be seen by the principal and other gatekeepers as clear evidence that the violator does not merit membership in the professional culture. This section discusses the findings on assumptive worlds.

All professions have informal, unstated rules about what one should believe and how one should speak and act. "The culture of a profession consists of its values, norms, and symbols" (Greenwood, 1957, in Vollmer & Mills, 1966, p. 16). Norms guide behavior by delineating an elaborate system of role definitions. Individuals (such as assistant principals) just entering a profession are acutely sensitive to those rules; they often learn the rules only when they receive a cold stare or a direct reprimand for violating one (Bosk, 1979; Schein, 1978).

The following description identifies the rules for assistant principals and their implications.

Right and Responsibility to Initiate

The assumptive worlds of site administrators include understandings about who takes initiative and exercises discretion. Traditionally, the principal, a district middle manager, must implement district policy having had little input into that policy (although this tradition is challenged by restructuring and site-based management reforms). The principal exercises discretion when assigning duties to the assistant; the duties may leave little opportunity for initiative and risk. Still, some assistants want to try out new ideas and gain visibility, but the rules of assumptive worlds limit that behavior.

Rule 1: Limit risk taking. Risks undertaken by assistant principals must improve the school without causing major changes or inviting strong opposition. Developing a curriculum to cope with a crisis— like the unresolved emotions from a student suicide—is one such example. One assistant developed a school newsletter and a popular new procedure for managing suspensions; such safe projects were particularly important because that assistant often had conflicts with his principal over substantive issues like the importance of academics compared with student activities.

Rule 2: Remake policy quietly. Site administrators can and often need to overlook, evade, or loosely interpret policies that do not work well for their school. (Karl Weick, 1982, notes that school systems are "loosely coupled," so looseness of monitoring and direct communication allow such flexibility.) In some situations, assistants find it necessary to quietly ignore or even defy the demands of the district or their principals.

In one instance, an assistant principal skirted around strict compliance with Public Law 94-142 rather than leave disabled students with an incompetent substitute. Another, faced with the need to placate a teacher with an ill-furnished room in the basement and follow bureaucratic rules about furnishings, tapped into her own network to get furniture delivered.

Such is the work of the street-level bureaucrats (Weatherley & Lipsky, 1977), who, when faced with chronically scarce resources and pressings demands, remake policy. Assistant principals learn to do this quietly.

Acceptable and Unacceptable Values

Assistant principals learn that certain values are the "right" values in their district and their school sites. Their speech and behavior must demonstrate adherence to these values.

Rule 1: Avoid moral dilemmas. Open and public displays of the tough issues must be avoided in administrators' assumptive worlds. For example, one junior high assistant had spent a lot of time counseling a boy, which resulted in tremendous improvement in his behavior and academic work. When a security guard provoked an altercation and reported the boy at fault, this assistant was tempted to make it a public issue. However, she understood the rules of the assumptive worlds and knew that she would jeopardize her promotion. She found a way to transfer the boy and kept the dilemma private.

Rule 2: Do not display divergent values. The assistant who is at odds with teachers, other administrators, and the power structure must avoid display of these conflicts. One inner-city high school assistant talked privately about his observation that "power and money don't give a damn" and "America is not going to support inner-city schools" (Marshall, 1985b, p. 132). However, when he aired those opinions, he displayed his defiance of the dominant values.

Patterns of Expected Behavior

Often assistants find out about the assumptive worlds' rules of behavior when they violate them.

Rule 1: Commitment is required. In the midst of a personal conflict raging among the superintendent, the athletic director, board members, and faculty factions, one assistant decided to remain aloof and uninvolved. He even declined the superintendent's offer to sponsor him in a social club. Not recognizing this as a call for commitment and loyalty, the assistant lost the opportunity for superintendent sponsorship.

Rule 2: Don't get labeled as a troublemaker. One upwardly mobile female assistant principal was ready to challenge her district's examination for principalships and demonstrate that the model answers were wrong. Fellow administrators told her to withdraw her challenge, even if she were right, because the resulting "troublemaker" label would ruin her career.

Rule 3: Keep disputes private. The junior high assistant who squealed learned an assumptive worlds lesson. She felt justified in demanding special repairs and maintenance for her "special school," but by provoking a dispute with the district engineer, she only got a lecture on following bureaucratic rules. If the dispute had stayed private and low-key, she might have received more help.

Rule 4: Cover all your bases. Assistants (especially those in vulnerable positions) must learn to rise up to every task and expectation held for them. A black female assistant (the only black administrator in a predominantly white, desegregated school) was particularly vulnerable. She was assigned semiclerical duties and was responsible for one-third of the teacher observations. But she saw a tremendous need to spend time counseling students and dealing with racial tension. Rather than earning her credit, this work pulled her away from her assigned duties, leading to a label of "inefficient."

School-Site Conditions Affecting Political Relationships

Each school site, even those in the same district, has specific turf and trust relationships that are part of its assumptive worlds.

Rule 1: Build administrator team trust. The assistant who has a partnership of trust, particularly with the principal, will receive support and commendations. One assistant, who was in a continuous intellectual and philosophical conflict with his principal, received not support but contempt. Even though the principal, teachers, and students relied on him and his work, this conflict undermined many of his efforts.

Rule 2: Align your turf. Site administrators understand that some tasks and projects are prized; others are considered "the pits." Discipline and repairs management may be undesirable responsibilities in one school but prized, essential tasks in another. The assumptive worlds lesson is this: Be sure to jockey into position to take charge of some of the prized tasks.

Implications of Assumptive Worlds

Detailing the assistants' assumptive worlds provides insight into the constraints within which they work. They are not to take initiative unless it is very likely to succeed. They are not to speak up about inappropriate policy—rather to remake it quietly. When they are upset about fundamental problems in schooling, they are to avoid any display of those dilemmas. Displays of loyalty, avoidance of trouble, smoothing over disputes, and fulfilling the clearly stated job description are more important than grappling with the tough issues of schooling. And the particularities of the site—whether or not assistants can build trust with their principal, whether or not they can gain some control over their task assignments—become key factors in assistant principals' satisfaction and success. The dilemmas in the assistant principal role were highlighted when Mertz (2005) observed assistant principals demonstrating loyalty for their principal, saying, "He's a nice man who would spend hours talking with a child to try to help him" (p. 21). But this is not enough when there is no vision for the school and more students are failing every year.

We are left with a picture of the assistant principal—the person entering the profession and learning how to be an administrator, the person who will be looked to for future school leadership—as a person learning to comply with dominant values, keeping quiet about fundamental problems, and taking few initiatives and no risks.

During the years since this research was done, these findings on assumptive worlds have stood the test of time. A recent communication with an assistant principal in Arizona (W. Walther, personal communication, October 31, 2004) lends validity to this, as he says:

- "If an assistant knows the absolutes (district rules regarding hiring, dismissals, evaluations, discipline, weapons, etc.), it is a much faster learning opportunity." (In other words, cover all your bases.) He illustrated this, saying, "Knowing that district policy for all drug cases was a 10-day suspension and a hearing, the hearing process, appeals, etc., I could manipulate a situation to my benefit and for the students, telling them I could help them prepare for the hearing—and, most important, I knew I had support at the site and district office."
- "It's all about working the system."
- "I knew that teacher evaluations could be overlooked . . . when push came to shove, evaluations took a back seat."
- "Do what the principal wants." (In other words, do not display divergent values; remake policy quietly.)
- He told of a former principal who would sweep many violations under the rug to avoid looking bad, which created conflicts for him.
- "I was shocked to see how business was conducted."
- Some principals had "no idea about some of the most basic procedures and policies with the district, and don't know how to address problems that need to be addressed consistently across the district," he said. (In other words, keep disputes private.)

An extreme example of assistant principals having to adhere to assumptive worlds' rules was reported in a news story called "Spared the rod, lost his job" (Dobbs, 2004). Ralph McClaney, a middle school assistant principal in Mississippi, refused his principal's order to paddle a sixth-grader who had acted up in class, saying, "The idea of a big white guy hitting an 80-pound black girl because she talked back to the teacher did not sit well with me." He resigned his $53,000 job rather than follow the order, saying that he quit knowing he would be fired for insubordination. The principal later said that his intention was to get students' attention, not inflict pain; that the state and district policy and advance parental consent allowed paddling; and that McClaney's decision to quit was a personal private matter.

In later research, Marshall (1992) explored the dilemmas and the values guiding site administrators. The sample consisted of assistant principals and principals who were chosen because they were different, in that they were "risk-takers," females, or minorities. They provided a range of vignettes of dilemmas, how they managed them, and what values guided their management. The dilemmas all revolved around the following:

- Dilemmas over asserting authority and enforcing bureaucratic rules (especially in their first weeks in the role, as they had to separate themselves from teachers);
- Dilemmas in supervising and evaluating teachers (especially in forcing retirements and in calling them on mistakes and unethical practices);
- Dilemmas stemming from helping children and solving societal ills (especially when the resources aren't available, as when a 14-year-old pregnant girl needed special help or when a district wouldn't allow a needed dental program for kids or an assistant to help a disabled girl to the bathroom); and
- Dilemmas arising from parent pressure (especially with parents who were upset about the "family life" curriculum or, for example, with the father who wanted to speak to the "real" school leaders, not a female assistant principal).

Of interest here: When asked what guided them in dealing with these dilemmas, these site leaders spoke of value systems formed by their upbringing, their religious values, and a general sense of fairness, caring, and openness. Few spoke of policies, codes of ethical conduct, laws, or university or other professional training.

Orientations to the Position

The same set of case studies was the basis for an analysis using career socialization perspectives, focusing on how assistants settle on an orientation to the career (Marshall, Mitchell, & Gross, 1994). Categories of orientation to the assistant principalship were identified from the case studies to assist in understanding the career process. These categories are as follows:

The upwardly mobile assistant principal. This person has developed a highly useful and active network of colleagues in professional organizations. This individual values loyalty to superiors and demonstrates a willingness to take risks. A "sponsor" has influence in assisting career goals.

The career assistant principal. This person does not wish to be principal but has created a pleasant working environment with preferred task assignments, good relations with higher administrators, and enough authority to view his or her position with pride.

The plateaued assistant principal. This individual would like a promotion to principal but has applied several times and been rebuffed. No opportunity has really existed for his or her advancement; such a person often lacks mentor assistance and the emotional intelligence necessary for good human relations.

The "shafted" assistant principal. This aspirant has fulfilled the criteria to be upwardly mobile but remains without a chance of promotion. He or she is plateaued and has lost a sponsor's help. Such a person may have lost out because of (a) inappropriate placement or (b) district changes. In addition, there may be acknowledged or unacknowledged errors, slights, or faux pas. In short, sometimes politics is the cause; but in litigious environments the errors or lapses may be outside the aspirant's understanding, and it is likely that he or she may never have a chance to respond to the charge. Nonetheless, the error or the perception will slow or extinguish advancement.

The assistant principal who considers leaving. This assistant principal is young enough to develop an alternative career and may have other skills enabling him or her to change professions and earn more money. This person may have been in a management position outside of education.

The downwardly mobile administrator. Research showed a reverse career trend for some assistant principals, from principal to assistant principal or teacher, or to principal of an elementary school from a secondary principalship. These reversals could be involuntary, with reduction in administrative staff due to budget or demotion due to a political mistake. Voluntary reversals in position were requested by principals with health problems or those who wished to return to a job with tasks they preferred.

Downward mobility is more likely to happen in larger school districts where parents would be less aware of the new administrator's background. This phenomenon also can be a very clear message to other administrators about behavior or errors. It should be noted that as administrative unions and associations grow stronger across the country, school districts may not be able to reduce salary in these demotions because of strong administrative contract language. In these cases, the demotion is more a vote of no confidence than a real hardship. Again, recognizing the ego of many administrators, this action may be enough to push an assistant principal toward resigning or at least looking to other districts for advancement.

Details From the Case Studies

The above six categories were developed from intensive case studies of 20 assistants. Themes in their careers are detailed below to show the career stories from which these categories emerged.

Perception of mobility. Most assistant principals perceived the position to be a transitional one in which to learn skills and prove oneself. Doris Schroeder, Martin Jameson, Ellen Carson, and Susan Rafferty are some examples of people who had clear visions of where they wanted to move in the future. Each set up a plan for systematically demonstrating as many skills as possible in school administration.

For example, Doris Schroeder taught high school in a district that was cutting back on personnel and closing schools. As president of her district's teacher's organization, she was asked by her superintendent to head a task force on reorganization of the district school curriculum and personnel. As a result of her recommendations, the district replaced a junior high school with a middle school and opened up two assistant principalships. Doris applied for one of the assistant principal positions and got the job, having received help from a woman who was then deputy superintendent. However, when the district leadership changed and Doris applied for an elementary principal position, she did not receive it. She expected to eventually become a principal or assistant superintendent in her district or one nearby.

Joan Dixon was coached by an assistant superintendent to apply and prepare for a districtwide supervisory position after teaching for seven years. She grasped this opportunity and later sought an assistant principal position with the advice of her mentor. She took on as many tasks as she could, even chairing district committees during a sabbatical year.

Martin Jameson planned to spend three years in teaching and then move up to administration. He followed his plan. He became an assistant principal and then sought a promotion to the principalship. He had a clear understanding of the local politics of his district and also applied in other districts. When he did not get the principalship of his high school or middle school, he accepted a principal-superintendent position in another small district. Then, three years later, he moved to a larger district as superintendent.

Ellen Carson took on any new task before her. She took the examination for the high school and middle school principalship after only two years as an assistant principal and was promoted to the principalship of an alternative school for challenged kids.

William Russell, an assistant principal for 13 years and in charge of his high school's annex, said, "There is nothing more I can learn in the position. Now I am afraid I'm stuck." Although he was on his district's principal list, he did not apply when the opportunity was there.

Passing the loyalty test. Assistant principals often face moral and ethical choices that demand decisions that will affect their careers. Failure to observe loyalty norms constitutes a social error (Bosk, 1979), which may disqualify an assistant principal from upward mobility. Loyalty errors include failure to support the boss, defiance of district orders, or publicly questioning superiors. Elizabeth Anderson openly defied her principal on a variety of issues and could be heard in the outer office arguing with him. David Greenberg openly criticized his superintendent over a salary issue and was told by an Administrators' Association member to retract his comments. Katherine Rhoads challenged her district's test answers after failing a principal-level examination. She was advised not to persist if she wanted a promotion. She then dropped the challenge.

Martin Jameson's Whitman School District was rife with conflict. He lost his chance to become principal of his high school by ignoring the superintendent's request that he join a certain service club (thereby failing the loyalty test). When the high school principal was demoted to a middle school position, Martin was a favored candidate of teachers and community. He declined the superintendent's club. Martin did not receive the principal position and applied elsewhere. He was offered (and accepted) a position as principal/superintendent in another district.

Sponsorship. Research shows that administrative careers develop in a sponsored mobility system (Marshall, 1979; Ortiz, 1982; Turner, 1960; Valverde, 1980). Sponsorship offers informal support, training, and an affective bond that assures the protégé the visibility, advice, and career direction needed to build a successful administrative career. Several case studies show how sponsorship can influence career outcomes.

When Joan Dixon was a teacher, an assistant superintendent advised her to take courses in preparation for an administrative career. With his advice, she moved into a language arts advisory position for a year and later into a high school vice principalship. She was aware of the importance of sponsorship and developed a network of potential sponsors.

David Greenberg at Robert Frost High School had applied for a principalship and been passed over on several occasions. He often vocalized his discouragement with the selection process and with some of the administrators he had observed. David's principal, Dr. Fergusson, recognized his value as an assistant principal with good ideas that he knew how to implement into programs. He perceived that David handled discipline well, was fair, and that students liked him. However, many teachers felt he lacked interpersonal skills. He was unable to gain a sponsor, as it appeared that he did not actively support the values of raising student "self-image" in a troubled urban school district.

Ellen Carson worked in the same district. As a new assistant principal at Longfellow High School, a model academic school, she took on tasks with enthusiasm and demonstrated her ability to accomplish her principal's goals. She risked initiating new record-keeping policies, which, although unpopular with teachers, were improved systems for student records. She was available to listen to teachers' concerns and to provide resources. Ellen also was highly visible in professional associations. She and her principal, Dr. Perkins, developed a trusting relationship almost immediately. Dr. Perkins had assumed his position as principal only two months before Ellen was assigned to Longfellow. He found the other assistant principal, who had been a candidate for Dr. Perkins's position, to be uncooperative. Thus he relied on Ellen's skills. Dr. Perkins gave Ellen a glowing personnel report when she left Longfellow High.

Both principals relied heavily on the talents of these two urban assistant principals, yet the responses of Dr. Fergusson and Dr. Perkins to the assistants' career aspirations were entirely different. Both principals praised the work of their assistants; however, Dr. Perkins acted as a sponsor and mentor for Ellen, while Dr. Fergusson did not act as a mentor for David. Dr. Perkins openly supported Ellen in public, encouraging her to try for a principalship in spite of her short term as a vice principal.

The absence of sponsorship can have a negative effect on one's orientation to the career. George Tiempo was the only Hispanic administrator in his small city district and had been responsible for obtaining federal grants and instituting bilingual programs in his district. Although he had a doctorate and felt overqualified as an assistant principal, his principal supported another candidate in the school for the principalship. George then applied for another vacant principal position but was unsuccessful. He had no apparent support from any sponsors during the selection period. His aspirations were so frustrated in his district that he considered leaving education, as he also had another successful career as a financial consultant.

Settling into the assistant principalship. Those assistant principals who were comfortable in their position admitted two things. They made conscious decisions to put their family first and to reject the time commitment incurred by the principalship. Rejection of the principal role also meant they were not interested in its inherently political nature.

Ralph Long found that the assistant principal position contained responsibilities exactly suited to his talents and preferences. After returning to the United States from a prestigious education position abroad, he held several administrative posts with little satisfaction. The assistant principal position at Devon High School, he perceived, "was ideally suited to me because it had to do primarily with curriculum and not discipline." Ralph became the highly respected instructional leader of his high school and only recently retired from this position.

Andrea Gibson defined herself as a career person, wanted time for her family, liked the way the job fit her personality, and rejected the pressures and time demands of the principalship.

A striking finding was that a large percentage of the men, 43 percent, elected to remain in the assistant principal position, while only one of the 13 women (8 percent) selected that position as her final career goal. We believe this is skewed from the general assistant principal population because the subjects were not randomly selected. Among the women who entered the administrative career in line positions, four aspired to move to central office staff positions away from line positions, but none of the men expressed any desire to take this career direction. In fact, George Tiempo, once in a bilingual staff position, moved to an assistant principal position to be better placed for a move to the principalship.

Gender as a factor. Many of the female assistant principals in the study observed that they were treated differently than their male counterparts. Jean King and Carole Mann were told outright by superintendents that women were not considered for principal positions in their districts. Jean then moved to another district, where she became a high school principal after two years. Carole outlasted her superintendent and became a principal after devoting 36 years to education. Alexis Clark was told by one of her principals, "I would never respect a woman as a leader."

Elaine Jones, a black woman appointed to a white male administrative team, was not invited to the informal team as a colleague. Susan Rafferty had a sponsor but felt that she experienced more testing from faculty because she was female and young. Both Ellen Carson and Doris Schroeder related stories of male colleagues attempting to undermine their authority as assistant principals and of male teachers who appeared unwilling to take direction from them because they were women.

Implications. Assistant principals develop orientations in response to the opportunities and tasks they experience during their time in the position. Upward mobility requires commitment to one's career and to the organization. In the assistant principalship, the individual has an opportunity to demonstrate commitment as well as positive skills and attitudes for the district.

The principal is an "insider" who has major control over the promotion process. Principals provide the resources for training experiences in the school as well as access to information sources and opportunities for visibility (Mitchell, 1987; Valverde, 1980). The relationship of the teacher-aspirant and the assistant principal to the principal is vitally important in the socialization process and in gaining the principal's support and sponsorship.

Career timing and planning, and the ability to define situations in which one can successfully take limited risks, are also major factors that promote or inhibit mobility. When positive factors are in harmony (the opportunity for promotion exists and the candidate has respected sponsorship)—and the candidate desires promotion—this predicts that the assistant principal aspirant should be upwardly mobile.

However, the research showed that not every assistant principal wants to move up the ladder or will receive the opportunity. In the case studies examined, it was evident that not all assistant principals had received the acceptance of the organization and the authority that Ralph Long enjoyed. Those who are up against an organization that plateaus or "shafts" the aspirant feel tremendous frustration.

Analysis of the contexts in the case studies shows that each district and school organization has its own norms and traditions. Each person developed a response behavior to a particular district.

The school culture imposes an uneven set of conditions, restraints, and opportunities on each assistant principal. The working environment has a profound effect on the attitudes and aspirations of assistant principals.

New Research Insights

The research on assistant principal socialization reported extensively above was carried out in the Northeast in the 1980s. Research from the 1990s into the new century shows similar patterns.

Factors Affecting Assistant Principals

Mertz's (2005) study of the organizational socialization of assistant principals in 2000 in a south central state found, in great detail, patterns similar to those in older studies. Strong and significant factors affecting assistant principals were:

- Assistant principals are defined by and learn from their duties;
- Principals control their work lives and their futures, determining what experiences the assistant principals are exposed to;
- In such contexts, assistant principals have little autonomy or decision-making power, and working as a team "does not mean cooperation or collaboration but 'doing your job' and 'staying in your own lane'" (p. 25);
- Being successful means being loyal and agreeing with the principal's way of doing things;
- Being an assistant principal can extinguish a disposition for change and innovation since "every time you go against the system you lose juice" (p. 29).

These school leaders' learning was reinforced "slowly and subtly, implicitly rather than explicitly, as an unconscious concomitant to the ongoing day-to-day work," through daily interaction (Mertz 2005, p. 32).

A FOCUS ON THE CAREER ASSISTANT PRINCIPAL

What motivates people who are comfortable staying in the assistant principalship? How do they make meaning of their lives? These questions were pursued in a study sponsored by the NASSP, using surveys, shadowing, focus group interviews, and in-depth interviews of 10 assistants, their spouses, teachers, fellow assistant principals, and principals (Marshall, 1992).

This research captures the interactions, the context-laden nuances, and the special nature of the assistant principal role. The report begins with a simple realization: "Career assistant principals are among the first people to arrive at school in the morning . . . once students begin to arrive, the career assistant principal starts walking" (p. 7). This simple observation acknowledges the power of the dedicated assistant principal to set the tone for the school culture and for the arriving students' day. This is the sort of research that uncovers the potential for shaping the role as satisfying work. Two quotes illustrate this: "I will firmly believe until the day I die that it has been my calling to deal with young people and to relate to them." "I don't really have a bad day . . . It's hard for me to have a bad day unless somebody comes in here with a gun" (Marshall, 1992, p. 7).

The findings are derived from research on 50 successful and content assistant principals who had been in administration an average of 15 years, with an average age of 49. Some had served under as many as 10 different principals. Participants' work settings represented 22 states and the District of Columbia and included every region of the country. Their school districts ranged from one rural area that encompassed a sparsely populated 160 square miles to cities the size of Anchorage and Little Rock. The observations of these individuals at work provide earthy and provocative insights into school life.

Locations. First, one sees the significance of locations. The assistant principal's office is full of posters with antidrug messages and plaques of appreciation, policy manuals, walkie-talkies, and file drawers containing staff evaluations, with caches of confiscated water pistols, plastic vomit, and other adolescent favorites. The corridors and cafeteria, full of noise and heat, are the locales for chatting with teachers and students. Banter with students about the food, their T-shirt messages, and yearbook pictures serves as a relationship-binder. To prevent student trouble, the assistant principal's job is sometimes "just being seen" (p. 10). At the elementary level the patrol is less about smokers and lovers and more about tears over spilled milk. Assistants' typical 8 to 10 interactions per minute help set behavioral expectations and bind relationships.

The grounds, the parking lot, and the wider community—which may include the local convenience store (source of the plastic vomit), the Rotary Club, and the bus drivers—are locations for further dissemination of the school's purpose. Assistant principals' spouses, like it or not, also get the job, as they are targeted in grocery stores and malls by parents with gripes.

Tasks and roles. Their years of experience give assistant principals the opportunity to take charge of their roles. They are quite accustomed to the huge diversity of tasks and the fast pace. However, they creatively carve out management techniques. Some write their own job descriptions, literally or by subtle understandings. Many, having seen for years the patterns of student discipline problems, devise individualized programs for diverting emerging violence or emotional tumult. Two quick examples are the basement punching bag for the angry 12-year-old boy and the special club for the kids with the most obviously awkward puberty challenges. These head off problems before they erupt.

Career Assistant Principals' Rewards and Satisfactions

Pleasures include:

- Sharing students' lives; as one said, "I get the biggest kick out of seeing problem kids shape up" (p. 24);
- Solving problems, e.g., having "the power to pick up the phone and solve a problem" (p. 24);
- Helping teachers, providing empathy, being instructional consultants, shaping those receiving bad evaluations; and
- Managing the culture, setting the tone, and being a force for stability.

Career assistant principals have more control over their personal lives than assistant principals who are on the move upward. When upward mobility requires lots of university work and moving family from district to district, missing too many of their own children's plays and basketball games, career assistant principals often choose to stay put. They maintain their family stability—and perhaps even a hobby!—and they avoid the principalship, seeing that "you literally have to be married to the building if you're going to do a good job as a principal" (p. 27). Interestingly, in another in-depth study, Mertz (2005) found assistants who had once sought principalships but now say, "I'm making as much as the principal without the aggravation" (p. 11).

Caring. Many career assistant principals view discipline—usually the most hated task for assistant principals—as caring for children. Thus this enormous task is transformed into an honorable mission. Career assistant principals know the policies but often exercise tremendous interpretive leeway as they act, quickly, as detective, judge, and jury, not only with students but with parents, teachers, and other staff. They recount numerous stories of elaborate individualized solutions to complex situations devised during their years on the job.

Discretion, flexibility, and freedom. Because of their long tenure, career assistant principals know how to push the limits of what is possible and what is allowed by policy. This creative power and freedom provides great pleasure.

Freedom means being able to avoid the visibility and the cross fires of controversies, even to make mistakes without great consequence. Unlike the principals they have known (and often trained), they "have a nice cushion, protected from the board and the superintendent" (p. 34). At the same time, a career assistant principal, while still being a team player, can be outspoken, bullheaded, and blunt when necessary to advance the program, the values, or the child for whom they are caring.

Stress management. The career assistant principal develops diversions (aerobics, woodworking, etc.) to cope with the hazards of the job, like high blood pressure, stomach problems, and weight gain. They also become philosophical about how their job works well for them—how it fits with values from their upbringing and their beliefs about helping, initiative, fairness, and caring.

Reflecting on the in-depth research on these career assistant principals and searching in research and theory for explanations, Marshall came upon the frameworks from feminist theory, which emphasize caring and relationship-building. She named her ensuing publication *Caring as Career* (1996) to demonstrate how the women and men who stayed on, reasonably satisfied with their work and with their lives, had placed their family stability, their relationships, and their valuing of caring first, not only for their personal lives but also in their vocation.

RESEARCH ON STYLES OF ACHIEVING

How do assistant principals work to accomplish their goals? Are some styles more valued than others? Could promotion rates of assistant principals with particular achieving styles indicate trends in preferred styles by senior administrators who are responsible for advancing administrative careers? One study asked these questions, with particular interest in race and gender. Informed by the critical theories in feminist research and the low numbers of women and minorities in the assistant principal ranks, Hooley (1997) wondered if the tide was turning and if those assistant principals, male or female, who reported a "relational" or more feminine style would be promoted more often than their nonrelational colleagues. In 1992, he asked 350 administrators (who had been assistant principals in 1982) to report on their styles using a self-report questionnaire. He also obtained reports from central office staff on the nine styles included in the questionnaire. By tracking assistant principal careers over the decade, focusing on their styles of achievement as well as race and gender, Hooley hoped to gather correlational information on who was getting promoted and what style was preferred. The Achieving Styles Inventory (ASI) includes nine styles on a continuum grouped into three larger categories or sets: Direct, Instrumental, and Relational (see Table 3.1).

The Direct Style Set relies most fully on the individual and is exemplified by go-getters, self-starters, and people who like to take charge and work independently. One might see this as the more traditional style among administrators and perhaps the more masculine. The Instrumental Set is the middle ground between the Direct and Relational Sets. These individuals prefer to work in groups; they advance networks and consider empowering themselves and others to be important in their work style. Finally, the Relational Set might be most closely aligned with the ethic of care (Noddings, 1992). They accomplish tasks by identifying with others and by adopting the goals of other people, institutions, or groups.

Overall about 63 percent of the sample (215 individuals) were promoted during the decade from 1982 to 1992. Not surprisingly, white males were promoted at the highest rate, but the effect was especially significant since they also accounted for 64 percent of the starting sample.

Again, predictably, nonwhite females, who represented only 3.7 percent of the total sample, saw a promotion rate of only 38 percent. This group has the double curse of being poorly represented in the assistant principal ranks and then promoted less frequently than both their white and nonwhite male and their white female counterparts.

Table 3.1   Lipman-Blumen Achieving Styles

Style—Indicator	Category
Intrinsic—excels	Direct
Competitive—out-performs	Direct
Power—takes charge	Direct
Personal—persuades	Instrumental
Social—networks	Instrumental
Entrusting—empowers	Instrumental
Collaborative—joins forces	Relational
Contributory—helps	Relational
Vicarious—mentors	Relational

In the second part of the study, the researcher tried to ascertain if particular styles correlated significantly with promotions. The results showed that the Relational Set and one of the Instrumental Styles were positively correlated with promotion, indicating that those who were promoted also were slightly more likely to be Relational in their style of goal accomplishment.

The third phase of the study involved collecting data from senior staff in two North Carolina school districts, one urban and one rural. These are the administrators who presumably have the most say in the selection and promotion of junior administrative candidates. They used an adapted version of the Organizational Achieving Styles Inventory. The urban senior staff favored Power Direct in ideal candidates more than their rural counterparts, but both favored the three relational styles highly.

Hooley's study is useful for identifying what happens as these people consider moving up in administration. It shows the variations in career ladder progress for whites and nonwhites and for women and men. Most important, it shows which styles are seemingly the promotable ones.

RESEARCH ON EMOTIONAL WORK

Strangely, little to no attention has been paid to the emotions of educators. In recent years, veering from the administrative science traditions, a few scholars have begun this line of research. In her ethnographic field notes, after her first day of shadowing a British head teacher (principal), Acker wrote, "Absolutely exhausting day . . . everything hurts. Have been up and down stairs . . . all day long. Constant onslaught of people and noise. Probably not typical?" (Acker, 1990, p. 251). Acker, in this and following work on deputy principals, demonstrated how from routines and events come stories, which can become "sagas" or "social dramas" from which deep meanings of schooling and leaders' work can be drawn. In particular, using feminist theory to evoke how "gender identities are socially constructed and confirmed through caring" (Graham, 1991, p. 67) and the emotional, relational, and caring aspects of educators' work, Acker spent 880 research hours in a small inner-city British primary school, one that was sometimes called "the hippie school" because of parents who believed in children being independent and assertive (Acker, 1999). She began with questions about educators' over-conscientiousness, about teaching as mothering, and about the mothering discourse in educators' work. The two deputy principals (with pseudonyms of Dennis and Debbie) felt mixed emotions and teetered on the edge of burnout because of the demands of caring. Acker, entering the setting as an observer, labeled the educators' work as "professional mothering" after seeing the nurturance of and bonding with children, the flexibility, the individualizing, and the coping with scarce resources.

In a study of leaders' emotions, Beatty (2000) includes one vice principal of a Canadian private school as part of her research sample. The positive emotions of leaders included:

- Creative flow, passion, excitement, determination, joy, high validation;
- Support, affirmation, sharing credit, supported in taking a risk;
- Self-affirmation when one's values and capabilities are sufficient, as when dealing with a pushy parent and balancing justice and care.

Negative emotions included:

- Disempowerment, feeling overwhelmed and discouraged, resentment when being controlled from above;

- Threatened by a critical and limiting boss;
- Having to be emotionally shut down, e.g., to an angry parent;
- Doing "dirty jobs" like deciding who will be fired, having to turn in a principal who has embezzled, and having motives questioned or being wrongfully accused in conflict-laden situations;
- Disillusionment from politics diluting one's best projects.

Themes emerged from the research on the vice principal, who told of being very angry with a student, a parent, and a teacher but said, "It's better to stay rational . . . to express your emotions of frustration at times through tears, or sadness, is okay" (p. 347), and that it was okay to feel anger but not to show it. She said that when attacked, she shut down. She said that fathers are more likely to "do a power anger thing" (p. 347), and she refused to be intimidated or to back down. She spoke of needing to feel connected with others yet in control of herself. She did recall working in a wonderfully supportive environment once, feeling "very safe. You could take risks" (p. 348). And she spoke of "sharing a student's joy with hugs" (p. 349).

AN INTERNATIONAL PERSPECTIVE

We should note that the plight of the assistant principal seems to be an international as well as an American phenomenon. One example can be found in a study of "deputy principals" in Queensland, Australia (Cranston, Tromans, & Reugebrink, 2004). A survey sent to secondary deputies was guided by previous research on roles and on concepts guiding the workload of deputies. Queensland schools range in size from 400 students (usually with one deputy) to up to 1,800 students with up to four deputies. The roles assigned to deputies are similar to those assigned to American assistant principals, although they demand greater involvement in instructional leadership and school-level change (Harvey, 1994). Reforms affecting these schools are similar to those affecting U.S. schools, although Australian devolution of power and responsibility to the site and increased emphasis on site-based management has greatly affected the deputy. Note some of the findings below and compare them with the findings and issues regarding the assistant principal in the U.S.:

- Respondents to the survey were 52 percent male and 48 percent female;
- Most worked in schools where there were two to three deputies; 85 percent worked 50 or more hours and 25 percent said they worked 60 or more hours per week;
- 80 percent were satisfied with their roles;
- Almost four in 10 intended to seek a principalship;
- Those not seeking promotion wanted to balance school, home, and family better and saw the principalship as too demanding and too focused on accountability.

Levels of satisfaction were greatly affected by the development of the notion of "team" among fellow administrators, in which principals and other members created relationships and skills for teaming. The most vexing dissatisfier was the lack of alignment between their ideal role and the real role. Ideally, these vice principals wanted to focus on strategic and curriculum leadership. In reality, however, they spent the bulk of their time on operational matters; student, staffing, and parent issues; and management. Their satisfaction was jeopardized by the "unrealistic demands placed on schools" (p. 234), especially with new policies and difficult students, principal turnover, expanded range of work, external agencies, changes in school demographics, and staffing issues, including poor teacher quality.

Deputy head, assistant principal, deputy principal—whatever the name, the issues seem very similar on the other side of the world!

SUMMARIZING INSIGHTS FROM COMPLEXITIES

In-depth research holds promise for describing the importance of assistant principals. It also identifies the fundamental dilemmas of school systems and how administrators cope. By watching and listening to assistant principals as they work with school systems, as they face these dilemmas, and as they question this system at the beginning of their administrative careers, we see the development of administrative coping mechanisms, values, and skills. Strong, complex forces socializing the individual into the culture of administration will not be changed by quick-fix alterations. Changes in the role will not work unless they accommodate such complexity.

This chapter compiles in-depth research that views assistant principals in their organizational context. It looks at satisfiers, emotions, and styles associated with the position and provides some clues about finding harmony in the job from research on career assistant principals.

DISCUSSION QUESTIONS AND ACTIVITIES

1. This chapter is based entirely on research. Some of it is from previous decades; some is very recent. Go through the chapter and mark the findings that seem similar to your own observations. Where the research and your own experience are different, discuss these differences.

2. Using the Internet and professional associations as resources, identify an assistant principal in another country and develop an electronic pen-pal correspondence, comparing roles, challenges, and insights.

3. Generate a debate about the barriers to discussion of assistant principals' emotions. From your own experience, what are your positive and negative emotions about your job? Cite some examples to share with others.

4. Generate a debate around this controversial topic: "Is the career assistant principal a loser or a valiant and balanced educator and human being?" Describe a career assistant principal you know who fits one of the two categories and explain why you see it that way.

5. Take some time to describe yourself or another assistant principal you've known who fits one of the various definitions discussed in this chapter. Tell stories and anecdotes to members of your group that indicate his or her placement in that category.

6. What is your achieving style? Do you think your achieving style has been an asset or a detriment to your career?

7. What prevents you from displaying your emotions on the job? Have you found ways to manage or sublimate the stress? What are your strategies?

8. Knowing what you do about the American assistant principalship, how would you expect the position to be different in other countries?

9. Given the research reviewed in this chapter, what study would you like to see done to help you with your work as an assistant principal? Do the case studies appeal more than the quantitative studies? If so, why?

10. Cite reasons to explain the paucity of deep research on the assistant principal.

CHAPTER FOUR

Opportunities for Improving the Assistant Principalship

T wo assistant principals, taking a coffee break, were grousing about how no one pays attention to what they do. One said, "What would happen if some wise and powerful people got together for a day for the purpose of improving our lot?" His friend replied, "That'll be the day!"

Actually, opportunities exist and a few policy, training, and reform efforts have been made to improve the lot of assistant principals. This chapter examines the status of current structures, programs, and policies that are areas of opportunity for improving the assistant principalship. It points out chronic problem areas and specific programs and policies. This chapter sets the stage for action to improve the assistant principalship and thus to improve schools. As the plight of public schools becomes more apparent to the general citizenry either because of the identification of failing schools through the NCLB legislation or because of the consistent barrage of test results and poor press, benefactors are stepping forward to help with training costs. The Bill and Melinda Gates Foundation has sponsored symposia in all 50 states to assist administrators in meeting the new challenges of public education with technology. Also, reforms in administrator licensure and refinements in university curricula and in district staff development sometimes give attention to assistants. Administrators' associations are also beginning to focus on assistants.

TRAINING AND CERTIFICATION POLICIES

The certification policies for all states are documented in volumes that are compiled and updated yearly by Elizabeth Kaye (2002). One can learn from these volumes whether their state certificate is valid in another state, how many and what kind of courses and tests are required for building-level and district-level certification, and even sometimes whether certain agencies or policymakers can grant exceptions. Educators can get up-to-date information about their state from the Web sites of their professional association and their state department of education. Most states, in fact, do not have separate specific certification requirements for assistant principals. With the increased rigor implicit in the language of NCLB calling teachers to be "highly qualified," state education departments are advancing a shift to similar standards for all administrators. In states like New York where the administrative tenure laws still exist, these laws are in jeopardy of being changed in order to increase administrative accountability. In the past, districts could "test" new administrators by having them serve as paid administrative interns before certification was complete. This is often no longer the case, and it will have a chilling effect on bringing new, diverse leaders into the administrative fold.

An analysis of requirements across the states reveals interesting patterns in the attention and intentions of state policymakers. Few states specifically mention the assistant or vice principal in the list of positions covered by administrative certification or have specific certification for them. Analysis of the requirements for entry into administration among the 50 states reveals a general policy of requiring a valid teaching certificate along with teaching experience and a master's degree in administration (or in another area but with educational administration courses) for administrative certification. Many require that candidates pass the School Leaders Licensure Assessment (SLLA) administered by the Education Testing Service. Some require *all* of these prerequisites; some require only the teaching certificate. Most states require teaching experience, some requiring at least three years. About half of the states require graduate training (ranging from six to 33 hours) in educational administration. States often grant the administrative certificate for a certain number of years, ranging from three to 10, so that it must be renewed. Renewal requirements may include taking courses and workshops as well as approval by the local superintendent. States have developed their own policy nuances. New Jersey, for example, requires for Provisional Principal Certification an offer of employment in a position and a comprehensive evaluation by a mentor. Maine does designate an Assistant Principal Certification; requirements include coursework in civil rights and Maine school laws, supervision and evaluation of personnel, and organizational theory and planning. Oregon also includes civil rights training as part of administrator requirements. Missouri has long, complex, and specific descriptions of requirements for educators but still lumps assistants in with principals. Mississippi gives administration master's-holding candidates an "Entry Level Administrator License" or they can take an "Alternate Route" with a master's of business administration, public administration, or public policy, along with passing several tests. Some states have their very own test, such as Florida's Educational Leadership Examination.

States may or may not have agreements of reciprocity with other states. Administrators who seek out-of-state positions may face the hurdles of taking courses and adhering to different certification policies even if they have attained certification in another state. In addition, many states impose requirements on new administrators, while incumbents are grandfathered in. It is still possible in some states to have a permanent certification (for example, in New York) if certification was received before February 2002. This is true for teachers as well. The more rigorous changes place still another barrier in front of aspiring administrators and contribute to the shortage of qualified and able candidates.

Clearly, state certification policies regarding assistant principals have not addressed the issue of specific training or requirements for the position. Thus school districts, professional associations, and universities are provided the freedom and the responsibility to create the training and standards for the assistant principalship. Many states, in their recent efforts to improve education through state policy, are currently proposing changes in administrator certification requirements.

There is an opportunity for altering and improving the assistant principalship by changing state certification policies—through sharper attention to requirements for periodic certification renewal, by requiring that university programs offer courses in supervision of staff development, by supervision of instruction, by equity policy, and by reciprocity agreements so that administrators can more easily move across state lines. Chapter 5 includes discussion of possible changes in certification.

University and Professional Training

Few opportunities exist for assistant principals to gain formal training for the position. Most learning occurs on the job, although the assistant principal can take general administration courses. This course description from Iowa State University may be the closest one gets to specific preparation:

Current Issues in Site-Level Leadership

Essential tasks of building-level leadership and management in contemporary school setting will be explored, including: curriculum and organizational structure, theory and practice of scheduling, financial management, roles and responsibilities of governance, communication and public relations skills, home/parental involvement and relationships, project and crisis management, technology integration, school climate and culture, effective student support programs such as counseling and guidance, attendance, and discipline.

In North Carolina, legislators and the State Board have created structures, supports, and requirements for training and internships. Universities with master's of school administration (MSA) programs admit teachers with high probability of entering administrative careers, and students have financial support for a year of full-time university coursework followed by a year that combines administrative internships with courses and, usually, real assistant principal positions. Such an approach combines the special capacities of universities with those of districts, state policy attention, and money.

The most useful university experiences provide reality-based training and a safe environment for experimentation with decision-making. For example, Schainker (2004) designed a master's comprehensive exam in which candidates are given a complex scenario describing a troubled school in a tough district and are graded as if their professors are members of a central office team selecting a new principal. They must show how they use their course work as they answer these kinds of questions:

1. Which are the most significant leadership challenges facing the school?

2. What specific activities would you initiate in the first three months? Which would you initiate later?

3. What specific types of assistance would you request from district officials . . . what would you do if that assistance was not provided?

This kind of exercise requires candidates to integrate their formal course work in a way that helps them assess their own leadership abilities. Done in the university setting, there is less of a "sink-or-swim" feeling for candidates who are still deciding whether they want to enter administration. At the University of North Carolina, Chapel Hill, students have requested specific skill-building in conversational Spanish and school law.

In rare instances, assistant principals may have a chance to participate in a workshop or a professional conference that addresses their particular concerns and provides skill-building experiences. Increasingly, semester-long internships are becoming typical. These experiences have the potential for very important learning for new assistant principals. Internship opportunities are hampered by the control issues of the principal who designs them. In the best cases, the interns substitute for assistant principals who are out of the building (at court or professional development sessions), working as part of the administrative team for at least one day. In other cases, the intern might be invited to evaluate a teacher along with the principal and then compare notes and attend the postconference. Clearly, the principal's comfort and confidence in his or her work dictates what is possible. It is common for interns to be given many duties or projects instead of opportunities to work as part of the team or practice teacher evaluations. For example, A. J. Mutillo's internship lasted for a full year, but he was assigned to one room supervising inschool suspensions, so, as he says, "It was a joke."

To what extent do these formal and informal training experiences help assistant principals anticipate the administrative roles, make appropriate career decisions, manage the tasks, and create an array of coping strategies for managing the dilemmas of their job in constructive ways? Do these experiences help them manage professional and bureaucratic conflicts? Do they build a sense of administrative professionalism? Do they provide rewards for the administrator who values instructional leadership, equity, and the use of research and theory to improve practice? There are few answers, but two surveys provide some leads.

Little has changed since the survey of all university educational administration programs belonging to the University Council for Educational Administration (UCEA) in 1984, asking whether they provided courses specifically for the assistant principalship. None did, and most did not offer courses on topics of importance to prospective assistant principals. Apparently the assumption is that courses for principals are adequate for assistants. Few assistant principals would agree with that assumption.

Another survey provides data. Marshall, Mitchell, and Gross (1994) surveyed a small sample of 42 respondents of NASSP assistant principal members in the 50 states. Only 29 percent of the respondents knew of any program or policy that aimed to improve the assistant principalship. The respondents' suggestions for improving training were focused primarily on preparing them for the problems that site administrators faced on a day-to-day basis, such as:

- Managing community relations,
- Discipline management,
- Staff evaluation,
- Program evaluation,
- Instructional management,
- Legal issues,
- Handling emergencies,
- Drug education,
- Computers,
- Facilities and fiscal management,
- Bus scheduling,
- Fund-raising, and
- Extracurricular supervision.

To address the assistants' specific task-oriented training, discipline management was the most often mentioned need, with some emphasis on the need for positive approaches to discipline. Few made comments about the skills and attitudes needed for assistants to cope in a vulnerable, ambiguous position in which one must carefully work within the assumptive worlds (as described in Chapter 3) and shape one's orientation to the career (as described in Chapters 2 and 3). Several respondents identified the importance of the principal in taking leadership to facilitate the assistant principal's development; several mentioned the need for ways to cope with "burnout" and with the reality of low incentive, no rewards, and lack of opportunity for moving out of the position, no matter how well one performs.

A recent survey (Bartholomew & Fusarelli, 2003) revealed assistant principals finding their course work very useful, finding tremendous value in their internships, and finding great value in their courses covering finance, school boards, and the superintendency. They also sought more career planning, resume development, effective public speaking skills, and interviewing skills. (It sounds like they were preparing to move up!) Assistant principals wished that their university training included more interaction with and teaching by building-level administrators.

Staff Development

Does staff development help? Most assistant principals have their hands full with all their duties and look askance at professional development distractions. Many educators grow cynical, having experienced staff development that has too little relevance to their particular needs. Good staff development directors and consultants elicit and assess needs ahead of time, including the district's strategic plan. But if a district has ignored the special nature of the assistant principal role in its planning, the cynical and busy assistant principals will have made good decisions in staying away. Too often, districts have only a shallow understanding of systemic staff development planning and rely "primarily on a rotation of external speakers who are among those considered 'on the cutting edge'" (Killion, 2002, p. 64).

Urban districts more than others are likely to provide a program to recruit and prepare candidates for the principalship (e.g., teachers and current assistants). But only one-fourth of districts do this, and the focus is on preparing and recruiting principals (Educational Research Service, 1998).

Reports of innovations offer useful models for improvement. In California's Santa Cruz County, where positions often had only two or three applicants and where assistant principals had only a narrow range of responsibilities, the district created a plan for viewing assistant principal and resource teacher positions as apprenticeships for principalships. Their "growing your own" approach has these features:

- Partnership with universities,
- Mentor/apprentice agreements and formal milestones for debriefing,
- Weekly and quarterly reviews,
- Variation in the tasks of assistant principals to broaden exposure,
- Help to thrive, not merely survive, and
- Assistant principals seeking further professional development opportunities.

The Capistrano, California, School District developed the Teaching Assistant Principal program, in which fledgling assistants, recruited by their site administrators, are given a range of leadership duties: developing curriculum, coordinating intervention programs, liaising with parents and community, and managing schedules and inventories. With a small stipend, they gain a master's and preliminary administrative credentials. They then become members of the management team, with duties like evaluating personnel, and they may apply for assistant principal openings. Capistrano's affiliation with a local university allows it to offer an in-house administrative credential (Lovely, 2001).

The School Leadership Initiative (SLI) was a three-year pilot mentoring program including participants from small rural schools bordering Mexico to urban high-poverty schools as well as more privileged schools (Zellner, et al., 2002). Participants were 70 percent female, 30 percent African American, and 10 percent Hispanic. A few findings are useful:

- Assistant principals need to engage in activities that go beyond the four Bs: bells, books, behavior, and bats (also known as the three Bs: books, butts, and buses).
- Administrators flounder when they are unable to spread leadership around, when they lack the ability to reflect on

their practice, when they lack experience in focusing on a vision for their site, and when they lack experience in self-initiated leadership activities.

- Administrators need to be mentored and supported during their initial stages of leadership development.

Recommendations for needs of teacher leaders and assistant principals include these:

- Opportunities to wrestle with real challenges in a safe environment under a principal's tutelage;
- Practice on leading collaboration;
- Reflection on practice;
- Principals obligated to mentoring;
- Active roles in curriculum and instruction;
- Principals must encourage effective dialogue, critique, and reflection, for "double loop learning"; and
- Professional learning communities, with common vocabularies, immersion, demonstrations, engagement, feedback, opportunities to learn from errors, and time to learn skills.

Assistant Principal Conferences

State-level conferences, often held yearly and often sponsored by administrators' associations, are an important improvement on the scene. A quick search on the Web shows one- or two-day conferences, specifically for assistant principals, in Washington, Texas, Illinois, Louisiana, Michigan, Virginia, Maryland, Kentucky, Alabama, and more. In some instances, such conferences are sponsored by large districts like Chicago or in venues like Southwest Texas State University. Typically, they cost the participant about $60 to $90 plus costs for special sessions, outings, and other extras. These conferences can "count" for professional development hours. Many include networking sessions, sessions on resume and interviewing skills, and job fairs.

Presenters include police officers, lawyers, experts on particular groups in special education, acting and retired principals and superintendents, and, in rare instances, scholars. Topics include crisis management, the assistant principal's role in meeting adequate yearly process standards, managing a diverse student body, communicating with parents, achieving staff buy-in for instructional leadership, handling tardies, safety, special education law, staff development and teacher evaluation, gangs, balancing personal and professional lives, "court-proofing your suspension and expulsion hearings," proper search and seizure, and so on. These topics reveal the particular kinds of on-the-job training that are attuned to the immediate needs of the assistant principal. Some conferences include the awarding of an "Assistant Principal of the Year." Indeed, the NASSP awards a national Assistant Principal of the Year at its national convention.

SELECTION POLICIES

Four decades ago, writing about administrator selection, McIntyre (1966, p. 10) said, "The challenge is one of finding or creating the situations that are really job-relevant and then recording and analyzing the candidate's behavior." He spoke of the problems of administrator selection, showing how the "trait approach" ignored the situational aspects of administration, how interviewing is judgmental, and how relying on letters of recommendation, transcripts, and rating scales is like reading tea leaves. This research and other studies along with growing shortages have led to the alternative credentialing movement, which has affected teaching certification as well as administrative licensure. Currently several large urban school districts are headed by nontraditional educational leaders. The assistant principal ranks have remained consistently tied to state certification standards as the first requirement in screening candidates. Interestingly, the policy rhetoric of the administration of George W. Bush has fostered this rigid selection criterion at all levels by coining the phrase "highly qualified" and applying it to teachers, teaching assistants, and substitute teachers. The issue raised in these other staffing areas decreases the likelihood that any great number of noncertified or nontraditional assistant principals will result.

Another factor affecting the homogeneity of the assistant principal candidate pool is that many professors of administrative courses are retired school administrators. As is the case with mentors, these professors are more likely to encourage and advance candidates who are most like themselves—usually white middle-class males with backgrounds in secondary teaching and administration. This further exacerbates the broad homogeneity of the assistant principal candidate pool.

Bridges and Baehr (1971) raised questions about the common use of administrator certification as the main selection criterion. They noted that the low participation of minorities in administrator certification programs would raise serious questions about the fairness of using certification as a criterion. More important, they challenged the very assumption that formal training will lead to greater effectiveness, showing research that indicated that traditional graduate courses may *lessen* administrator flexibility and that courses on the content of administration were unrelated to administrative success.

Since those challenges and cries of alarm were issued, there have been several innovations in selection processes, and attempts have been made to avoid using formal practices that unfairly discriminate. In addition, some selection processes include assessments for predicting candidates' future behavior as it relates to the job.

Assessment centers. The armed forces' sociometrics (peer ratings) and situational performance tests were developed to select military leaders, and the procedures have been translated for selecting educational leaders in assessment centers. Following this tradition, the NASSP, using consultants and job analysis experts, developed assessment centers as devices for making selection and promotion decisions for educational administration positions, primarily for principalships. NASSP provides setup and assessor training for districts that want centers. For candidates, this offers feedback useful for planning career goals and, for districts, an independent assessment of candidates aspiring to leadership, a way of identifying prospective principals, and data useful for planning professional development. To date, no job analysis and center training has focused on the assistant principal role.

Candidates, performing one half-day of exercise simulations (such as "in-basket" exercises, conducting performance evaluations, reporting to directors, and interaction with a parent and teachers), are evaluated as they display their skills. Decisions about the relevant skills to be assessed were made, in part, within the frameworks of the National Policy Board for Educational Administration, the Interstate Leadership Licensure Consortium, and the National Council for the Accreditation of Teacher Education skill domains (NASSP,

Table 4.1   NASSP Assessment Center Skills to Be Assessed

Skills	*Selected Illustrative Criteria*
Educational Leadership	
1. Setting instructional direction	Articulates high performance expectations
2. Teamwork	Seeks consensus
3. Sensitivity	Expresses recognition of feelings of others
4. Development of others	Shares expertise
Resolving Complex Problems	
1. Judgment	Sees relationship among issues
2. Results orientation	Acts to move toward closure
3. Organizational ability	Monitors progress
Communication	
1. Oral communication	Uses proper grammar and pronunciation
2. Written communication	Writes appropriately for different audiences

2005). Table 4.1 outlines the skills areas to be assessed and provides illustrations of selected behaviors expected.

Using analyses from six trained assessors, a report is produced for each candidate. Candidates' capacity on each skill is reported on a continuum, from "Derailer," which means "significantly detracts from performance," to "Noticeable Problem Area," to "Development Zone," to "Competency," to "Strength." Also, for each skill the report provides performance ratings in each of the six assessment activities, with "behavioral examples" of the candidate demonstrating the skill (or not). Finally, reports provide "developmental suggestions" that range from helpful hints and work management strategies to recommended readings.

The assessments are costly but are still used in some major cities and several states. Districts evaluate the NASSP center process and decide whether the expense and effort is worthwhile. Assessment centers have been critiqued, evaluated, and refined. Districts could use them as tools to actively select and promote a new and different leader, if their standards and selection processes included imaginative additional criteria. Districts could also use them as tools to limit access to the select few nominated. In the early center years, non-whites did less well than whites, men did slightly less well than women, and individuals serving in nonteaching roles (counselors or education specialists) performed better than their teaching colleagues (Schmitt, et al., 1984). Recent trends show that elementary school women perform the best, typically women do better than men, and data on performance by race are not tracked (L. Reed & W. LeGrand, personal communication, September 19, 2005).

Counties and districts reported that people who scored well in assessments also performed well on the job, sometimes predicting administrator success better than traditional interview processes (Gomez, 1985). NASSP has used job analysis research and two validity studies in 1979 and 1991, and they report that the process shows considerable predictive validity.

One of the authors (Hooley) went through this type of exercise in the Winston-Salem/Forsyth County Schools in North Carolina in the late 1980s. The school district at that time would have served an average daily attendance of about 30,000 students. In this case, the assessment was an in-house effort and the assessors were members of the senior staff, the central office administrators, and the building principals. Aspiring assistant principals were ranked based on their performance, but candidates were never led to believe that the assessment had any real effect on the selection process. Feedback to the aspiring administrators was limited and gave a score, but it did not indicate one's rank relative to other aspirants. The effort probably was an attempt to hire more internal candidates since the assessment was offered only to current employees.

Although Hooley later found that he was highly ranked on the assessment, others with low scores were also advanced to administrative posts without regard to their rankings. The effort lasted only as long as the assistant superintendent over personnel remained in her post. After that, the assessment was abandoned. The assessment in this case was a useful exercise, but it did not eliminate candidates from consideration. Interestingly, the person responsible for the effort was the lone female assistant superintendent in the organization. One might speculate that this was her attempt to bring diversity to the administrative hiring procedure. The assessment center concept is a good one when scores are used to screen applicants. This, of course, would need policy or regulation authority.

In the end, universally tight budgets in public schools nationwide have limited these efforts as they have reduced professional development opportunities for new and aspiring administrators. With NCLB demanding more before- and afterschool tutoring from school district coffers and similar policy squeezes on budgets, expenditures for administrative assessments are likely to be considered "frills." The abiding shortage of administrative candidates further minimizes the usefulness of such efforts.

Identifying competencies, standards, and tests. To assess an individual's potential for administration, tests can be useful. States have developed their own. Georgia's Test in Administration and Supervision focuses on these kinds of items:

- Demonstrate an understanding of the structure and governance of local school systems.
- Demonstrate an understanding of school safety regulations.
- Select the appropriate approach for evaluating instructional outcomes in a given situation.
- Identify strategies and techniques for solving problems related to school/community relations (Georgia State Department of Education, 1983).

The test included (a) an overview of leadership in education (e.g., delegation of authority, implementing changes, ethics of school administration), (b) organizational and legal structure in education (e.g., landmark cases, structure and governance of local school systems), (c) management of school operations (e.g., transportation, space utilization), (d) personnel management (e.g., student records, staff evaluation), (e) instructional supervision (e.g., basic teaching models, teaching/learning resources), (f) curriculum development (e.g., evaluation of curriculum), and (g) social issues in school administration (e.g., student rights, public relations). An analysis of five years of tests revealed that females consistently had a higher pass rate than males. Blacks had a low pass rate compared with whites (Schnittjer & Flippo, 1984). Testing is controversial and subject to court challenges when it differentially affects minorities.

Nevertheless, in the 1990s, in an effort to create national statements for competencies to be used (or not) by state standards boards, the Interstate Standards for Leadership Licensure (ISLLC) created

Table 4.2   Interstate Standards for Leadership Licensure (ISLLC)

A school administrator is an educational leader who promotes the success of all students by:

Facilitating the development, articulation, implementation, and stewardship of a vision of learning that is shared and supported by the school community.

Advocating, nurturing, and sustaining a school culture and instructional program conducive to student learning and staff professional growth.

Ensuring management of the organization, operations, and resources for a safe, efficient, and effective learning environment.

Collaborating with families and community members, responding to diverse community interests and needs, and mobilizing community resources.

Acting with integrity, fairness, and in an ethical manner.

Understanding, responding to, and influencing the larger political, social, economic, legal, and cultural context.

---

standards. These are now being used in many states' licensure processes and have been converted into a test administered by the Education Testing Service. Table 4.2 lists the ISLLC standards. ISLLC is a well-intentioned effort, and it does incorporate language about diversity, community, shared visions, and the like.

Increasingly, districts develop their own systems for performance appraisal, for training new principals, and for selection with state-level oversight. Again, budget constraints and pressures from the many unfunded mandates endemic in the NCLB legislation have likely slowed many of these initiatives.

Thus we see that attempts at defining tasks and skills and formalizing the selection process are signals of progress toward eliminating reliance on word of mouth and the "old boys' network" and toward making selection closely tied to job functions. However, these attempts have not solved persistent problems such as the shortage of good educational leaders, the stifling of innovation, the low representation of women and minorities in school administration, and more. These new approaches do not raise fundamental questions about the viability of old methods of recruitment and selection. They

do little to address the fact that assistant principals cope with fundamental dilemmas and learn to work within the confines of assumptive worlds, limiting their initiative and their values to fit within the
dominant ones. These new processes will do little to recruit leaders
who will meet the critical needs of an increasingly diverse student
population.

INSTRUCTIONAL LEADERSHIP

There are no widespread policy proposals supporting assistant
principals' involvement as instructional leaders. The array of assistants' tasks actually distances them from curriculum and instruction.
Yet the assistant principalship could be made into a position in
which instructional leadership qualities and skills are supported. The
literature on "effective schools" has emphasized the importance of
the principal functioning as an instructional leader. Bossert, et al.
(1982, p. 21) found that principals in effective schools devote more
time to "the coordination and control of instruction, and are more
skillful at the tasks involved. They do more observations of teachers'
work, discuss more work problems with teachers, are more supportive of teachers' efforts to improve . . . than principals in less effective schools." This effective-principal research gives only a vague
description of "instructional leadership behavior"; we still need to
know how principal behavior leads to school effectiveness. What
influences a principal to be oriented toward instructionally effective
behavior? How does the assistant principalship function in facilitating instructional leadership? Is it possible and/or wise for the assistant to exercise leadership in the instructional program? If so, under
what conditions does this happen and with what results? Does being
an assistant principal help or hinder a person in learning effective
instructional leadership behavior? Does an assistant principal forget
the orientation to instruction and to teacher needs while serving in
that position? What instructional background has prepared the assistant principal to evaluate instruction and to lead curriculum change?
How useful is experience in physical education or music instruction
to an assistant principal who is offering feedback on a classroom
lesson in calculus or French III?

Unfortunately, few studies to date have focused on the assistant
principal and instructional leadership. Of course instructional
leadership can emanate from people other than administrators. In

one study of four high school assistant principals who had reputations as instructional leaders, Gross (1987) found evidence that these administrators' predispositions to instruction did help them move from the classroom into administration. However, that predisposition did not provide support for their moving into higher positions; sponsorship was still the critical support needed for career movement. Furthermore, their principals' power and propensity to shift their tasks (even when they had clearly stated job descriptions) and the ever-pressing need to manage discipline undermined these assistants in their efforts to focus on curriculum and instructional issues. The one assistant who was able to focus on instruction was quite atypical. First, he had stated explicitly upon taking his job that he would not work on attendance or discipline. Second, he and the other administrators at his school worked autonomously. Third, there were four assistant principals in addition to the principal at this site. Fourth, he was content to remain in the assistantship and made no effort to move up in the career hierarchy. These are rare circumstances. Porter (1996) found that assistant principals in Maine do not identify themselves as instructional leaders but rather as the person who makes the school run efficiently, focusing on daily operations. We doubt this is merely a Maine phenomenon.

Recent research indicates that working with new teachers and helping teachers create lessons were the most rewarding parts of assistant principals' jobs (Bartholomew & Fusarelli, 2003). This research also revealed that the task of getting experienced teachers to change their traditional methods of teaching was a huge challenge. A majority of these assistant principals did say that they received considerable support from staff developers and professional development, which helped with their instructional leadership.

People report that they enter administrative careers for reasons that sound like instructional leadership: wanting to provide effective leadership, to have an impact on program quality, to be of service to children, to work with teachers in school improvement efforts (Shen, Cooley, & Ruhl-Smith, 1999). The data used by Shen, Cooley, & Ruhl-Smith (1999) were actually gathered in 1989. However, more recent research muddies the waters. The findings of one experiment raise questions. Winter and Partenheimer (2002) had 168 teachers and graduate students react to two versions of an assistant principal job. One emphasized the traditional role of discipline. The other emphasized instructional leadership. Teachers did not view the instructional leadership focused role as more attractive. The researchers concluded that "the general pool of teachers views the job of assistant principal as unattractive even if the job is configured to focus on instruction" (p. 19), and this finding held true even for teachers who were admitted to an administrator certification program! Thus we cannot simplistically declare that assistants should focus on instruction and curriculum. We must consider the realities of pressing tasks, the principal's power to alter task assignments at will, and the career consequences.

ACHIEVING EQUITY IN ADMINISTRATION

Women and minorities do not attain assistant principalships as readily as white males. The traditional view of the assistant principalship, which emphasizes discipline, facilities management, and supervision of extracurricular athletic activities, defines it, according to stereotypes, as a job inappropriate for women.

Remarkably, no one knows how many assistant principals in the U.S. are women or minorities. Therefore, this section must refer to data from the 1970s and data on principals and other administrators, as displayed in Tables 4.3 and 4.4.

We present recent data on principals, since recent and reliable statistics on assistant principals are unavailable. As Table 4.4 shows, the principalship is still predominantly male and Caucasian, but there have been some shifts.

Here are several additional interesting statistics on the 83,790 public school principals in 1999–2000:

- Male Caucasians' average prior teaching experience was several years less than that of females and African Americans;
- Only 1.9 percent held only a bachelor's degree and more than 54 percent held a master's degree;
- Eleven percent of females and 9 percent of males held doctorates;
- There was a substantial rise in the number of principals younger than age 40 from 1993 to 2000;
- The rise in number of principals older than age 55 was even greater—more than 18,000;
- The number of principals increased from 79,618 to 83,790 between 1993 and 2000.

Table 4.3 Percentages of Women and of Minority Women and Minority Men by Ethnicity in Selected Administrative Positions in Public Elementary and Secondary Schools, 1974, 1976, and 1978

Subgroups	Principals			Nonteaching Assistant Principals			Consultants/ Supervisors		
	1974	1976	1978[a]	1974	1976	1978[a]	1974	1976	1978[a]
Percentage of women	12.7	13.0	13.3	18.5	18.3	22.2	50.4	51.6	54.6
Percentage of minority women	2.2	2.6	2.8	5.1	5.4	5.4	9.3	11.0	11.0
Black women	2.0	2.3	2.4	4.7	4.8	4.7	7.8	8.7	8.3
Hispanic women	0.1	0.2	0.3	0.3	0.4	0.6	1.2	1.7	1.9
Asian women	[b]	[b]	0.1	0.1	0.1	0.1	0.2	0.3	0.4
Native American women	[b]	[b]	0.1	[b]	[b]	[b]	0.1	0.3	0.3
Percentage of minority men	7.1	7.6	7.3	12.7	13.6	13.8	4.8	5.0	5.4
Black men	5.7	5.8	5.6	11.0	11.4	11.4	3.5	3.5	3.6
Hispanic men	1.0	1.3	1.3	1.2	1.8	2.0	1.0	1.1	1.1
Asian men	0.1	0.1	0.1	0.2	0.2	0.2	0.1	0.2	0.5
Native American men	0.1	0.4	0.3	0.2	0.2	0.2	0.1	0.2	0.2

SOURCE: Equal Employment Opportunity Commission (1974, 1976, 1978).

NOTE: Percentages may not sum to subgroup total percentages because of rounding errors. Mail questionnaires were sent to stratified samples of school districts with 250 or more students.

a. These percentages are estimates because data are not included for several large school systems.

b. Less than .05%.

97

Table 4.4   Selected Characteristics of Principals in Public and
Private Schools, 1999–2000

Selected Characteristics	Total: 1999–2000
Total	83,790
Men	47,130
Women	36,660
Race/ethnicity	
White, non-Hispanic	68,933
Black, non-Hispanic	9,239
Hispanic	4,236
Race/ethnicity	
Asian or Pacific Islander	659
American Indian or Alaska Native	633

SOURCE: U.S. Department of Education (2002).

For contrast, private school principals (totaling 26,231 in 2000) were more likely to be women than men. However, their salaries were $23,000 less than public school principals.

Many women who aspire to administrative careers are convinced that stereotypical thinking about women's roles and about the traits required to perform on the job is the major barrier for them. In fact, Table 4.3 supports this perception for the 1970s. It shows that male minorities are able to attain the assistant principal position; one position in seven was held by a minority male in 1978. Women and minorities have difficulty finding sponsors because so many potential sponsors are white males who are more likely to identify with people like themselves. Has this changed? Why are data to answer this question not available?

Questions of competencies are raised, even after extensive research and experience should silence them. Long ago, numerous reviews documented the extensive research demonstrating women's competencies for administration (Marshall, 1989).

There are no comprehensive studies on women and ethnic minorities in the assistant principalship, but studies on the principalship can provide insights. Lovelady-Dawson (1980) summarized research literature that showed that (a) minority principals are most often found in schools with more than 20 percent minority population, (b) minority women suffer doubly because sponsorship is so crucial and most sponsors are white males, and (c) "minorities who persist in administrative aspirations take longer to advance than their majority counterparts." She pointed out that "minority principals, no matter how well trained, experienced, and dedicated, may face many barriers to effective performance arising from confused role expectations—such as being a spokesperson for the minority community, punitive disciplinarian, or defender of minority causes—that affect minority principals' relationships with their faculty and staff, their students and the community, and the local superintendent and school board" (Lovelady-Dawson, 1980, pp. 21–22).

People often judge the same work behaviors differently when displayed by male and female administrators. In a rather large study of teacher job satisfaction as related to principal leadership style, female principals are more active, interested, and involved in the classrooms than their male counterparts. Female teachers welcome this, but male teachers "are more likely to interpret the same behaviors as intrusions into 'their' domain" (Lee, Smith, & Cioci, 1993, p. 170). Male teachers generally do not accept the more participatory and less bureaucratic and managerial leadership often exhibited by female administrators. The researchers suggest, too, that an "in-group bias" may also orient men against women leaders. That is, men have been well served by a system in which their own gender dominates the principalship. Indeed, men have been favored and supported by male leaders in their attempts to rise to administrative positions. It could also be that men are likely to harbor some fear that when women occupy leadership positions, men will lose their advantage (Lee, et al., 1993, p. 172).

As "culture-bearers," minority administrators become the representatives of their ethnic group, with the duty to educate others about their cultural heritage (Hughes, 1988). Black administrators must perform competently while overcoming negative stereotypes. Hispanic administrators are grouped together even though the

Hispanic community includes diverse sociocultural and political subgroups and different histories of integration and immigration. The Hispanic administrator has the task of translating the culturally different values and interactions of his or her group while working in the predominantly Anglo-Saxon administrative culture. Native American and Asian American administrators, too, have the task of representing their cultural groups (even though they are diverse) and translating the dominant culture.

Another literature review by Haven, Adkinson, and Bagley (1980) revealed that ethnic minority administrators often lost their jobs or were demoted during school consolidations that were responses to desegregation and/or economic constraints. For example, the number of black principals in Texas declined by 600 between 1964 and 1970; the number in Delaware declined from 50 in 1964 to 16 in 1970.

In an extensive examination of literature on women in educational administration, Ortiz and Marshall (1988) showed that women were doing everything necessary to exhibit competence but still were not able to attain the top positions in administration. In 1980, fewer than 1 percent of superintendents were women. Ortiz and Marshall showed that the number of women earning educational administration degrees increased from 68 in 1955–1956 to 555 in 1981–1982, but women constituted only 8 percent of all professors of educational administration. These facts show that the efforts and results for sex equity in educational administration had not been effective in the era immediately after sex equity laws were passed. Laws to forbid sex discrimination are inadequate; the norms and structures of educational administration are too powerful and the few women who dare to sue may be committing career suicide.

Ambiguous and subjective methods for training, selecting, and interviewing allow subtle sex discrimination. Women's background experience (e.g., such as being president of a community volunteer group or drama club coach) may be deemed less valuable than the more obvious and traditional experience of the male football coach. The network spreads news of prospective job openings more effectively than do formal announcements. Often an "acting" male administrator is on the job right after the position is posted. Furthermore, sponsors are usually male, and they tend to groom protégés who are most like themselves.

Women's awareness of professional norms of loyalty prohibits their use of court action. As shown in Chapter 3, exhibitions of loyalty are essential; filing a lawsuit against the school board, the principal, or the superintendent is considered disloyal. Little activist support is available from professional associations like the American Association of School Administrators and the National Education Association; their activities to promote sex equity are primarily educational and, sometimes, include networking. Finally, monitoring and enforcement of laws against sex discrimination are weak to nonexistent. Funds and expertise for implementing Title IX and for equalizing curriculum materials (e.g., the Women's Educational Equity Act) are always inadequate and threatened.

The assistant principalship is a key position on the administrative career ladder. When women have unequal access to the position or when, on obtaining the position, they have less opportunity to do the tasks that prepare them to move up, the assistant principalship becomes a position that perpetuates inequity. Principals exercise powerful control over those assignments. Several in-depth studies (Marshall, 1979; Ortiz, 1982) have shown the importance of identifying the informal structures and norms that create subtle barriers to women who consider administrative careers. These studies, as well as that of Gaertner (1980), emphasize the importance of having sponsorship and support in initial career experiences. Also, the experience in the initial administrative position is key in determining whether an individual will aspire to and succeed in attaining higher administrative positions.

McCarthy and Zent (1982) found a large number of women and minority men among all administrative "recent hires." Almost half of the elementary principal and more than half of the elementary assistant principal "recent hires" were women. However, women were making far less progress in secondary positions and central office line positions leading to the highest leadership positions. Thus optimism must be tempered by the realization that progress will not necessarily lead to equal representation of women and minority males.

McCarthy and Zent were pleased that "the male/female ratio among recent hires (65/35), although still discrepant, indicated that progress has been made in bringing female representation among administrative personnel closer in line with the proportion of women in the national work force" (McCarthy & Zent, 1982, p. 24). However, the teaching workforce of educators is predominantly female, so simple equity (not affirmative action) should result in 50 percent to 80 percent of new administrators being female.

Since the McCarthy and Zent (1982) study, several sociopolitical phenomena have occurred with regard to affirmative action and women's rights. Successive Republican Congresses have repealed any shred of affirmative action, particularly for minorities but for women as well. The best-selling book *Backlash* (Faludi, 1991) explored a national retrenchment on progress for women in social, political, and employment issues. Hooley's work (1997) reflected this failure to promote minority females among secondary assistant principals who worked in North Carolina between 1982 and 1992. Males, white and nonwhite, and white female assistants were all promoted at 61 percent or better, but nonwhite females during the same period were promoted only at a 38 percent rate. This is partially explained by the small number of nonwhite female assistant principal respondents working in the state in 1982—only eight individuals! Unfortunately, federal oversight, special programs for women and minority males, and legal enforcement of affirmative action waned in the 1980s and 1990s.

Equity has not been accomplished, and the assistant principal-ship remains a crucial position for effecting equity. Even if there were powerful forces for equity, Table 4.4 demonstrates that the equity problem will not go away with small changes. Now, administrators' associations and the federal government do not even pay enough attention to collect new data on the status of women and minorities in the assistant principal position! Data from 1993–1994 reveal women occupying 34.5 percent of all principalships and 58.9 percent of elementary principalships. Secondary principalships were more rare for women. In those same years, blacks and Hispanics held 10.1 percent and 4.1 percent of the principalships, respectively.

More recent data on principals reveal that 43.7 percent were women and 17.8 percent were minorities (Gates, et al., 2004). This is some improvement over the data from the late 1980s, which showed that 87.5 percent of all school administrators were white, 95 percent of all superintendents were male, and 73 percent of all principals were male (Jones & Montenegro, 1990). Still, this is unremarkable progress. Equity will not be achieved easily.

Beyond the equity issues, there is the issue of students needing role models. Girls and minority children need to see people who look like them enacting leadership so that schooling teaches that they, too, can be senators, CEOs, and president. Perhaps more important, minority and female students and parents, especially single mothers, are more likely to create partnerships with administrators who share their gender and background. They are also more trusting of administrative decisions from such individuals. As schools become populated by increasing numbers of students in families led by single mothers and as the population in public schools is composed of more people of color, this deficit is worrisome.

Ironically, the crisis in recruiting new administrators to increasingly stressful jobs opens opportunities. A few districts have jumped at the quick fix of hiring noneducators in superintendent and even principal positions, even though 90 percent of principals report that their teaching experience was highly valuable to their success as principal (Fenwick & Pierce, 2001). A far better option will be to alter the role and the recruitment and support of teachers who would consider the administrative jobs if they were redefined and more supportive of underrepresented groups.

SATISFIERS, SUPPORTS, AND COPING STRATEGIES

"Running, working out, having two comrade assistant principals who really understand—the teachers don't and the principal has her own challenges"—these are the de-stressors fashioned by A. J. Mutillo in his second year as assistant principal. The three assistant principals joke about "Ben and Jerry days," when sharing ice cream together seems the best way to shake off the stress.

Assistant principals' ways of managing challenges, finding support, and achieving satisfaction vary. In a study of assistant principals, Yee (personal communication, May 30, 2003) found two who commuted 100 miles a day but made good use of the time to prepare mentally for the day and to process the day's activities. Family support appears to be key to survival and to considering advancement. Most agree that the assistantship is a stepping-stone to higher administrative posts, but several declined their first principalship offers when the school was too difficult, when they felt they needed more experience, or when the personal commitment required just did not fit their current situation.

Years ago a study of assistant principals focused on the question of job satisfaction and tasks and roles. Croft and Morton (1977) found that 48 percent of assistant principals in Houston and 39 percent in Kansas reported, "I am not satisfied with my present position and plan to seek another position" (Croft & Morton, 1977, p. 25).

As a way of understanding role satisfiers, Croft and Morton asked assistant principals to rate job tasks on a scale. They found that tasks of greatest satisfaction were those relating to school public relations programs and informing the public of the school's achievements; developing orientation programs for teachers and students; and responsibility for teacher selection and evaluation, pupil attendance, and varsity athletics. Such tasks are related to areas for which the assistant principal was academically prepared and that require unique skills and ability.

Assistant principals said that such tasks as field trips, innovations, and pupil discipline were only slightly satisfying. They found little satisfaction in the tasks that required a lesser degree of academic preparation and ability, such as transportation services, student photographs, nonschool building use arrangements, and clerical tasks.

The researchers concluded that the highest satisfaction was to be found in duties that required a higher degree of expertise and administrative ability than those clerical-related items. Satisfaction, therefore, becomes a function of the degree of skill and ability that is perceived in the performance of a task by assistant principals. The higher the professional skill and ability perceived, the greater the satisfaction (Croft & Morton, 1977, p. 57).

Practitioners offer advice to help assistant principals find satisfaction in their positions. In 1980, the *NASSP Bulletin* published articles about defining the position by identifying competencies; by clarifying the role and using time management strategies to alleviate stress; by working toward a team approach; by creating formal evaluation processes that are based on the roles, tasks, and values of the school; and by asserting principles for assistants. However, we have no evaluations or studies to indicate whether such approaches do indeed help. Does a strictly set job description help an assistant principal cope with role conflicts, or does it hinder action in crises and get in the way of educators working as teams? Are assistants more satisfied when they are evaluated frequently on stated, formal criteria, or do they find they can accomplish more, both for the school and for their own self-development, by having flexible, wide-ranging responsibilities? We can gain some insights from the oft-studied principalship in raising these questions.

For principals, discretionary power is important. Crowson and Porter-Gehrie (1980) found that urban principals use areas of discretion to perform crucial functions for their schools. Principals, faced with ambiguous roles and scarce resources (e.g., time, information, personnel, and technical expertise), must cope by making quick decisions, doing surface monitoring of implementation of policy, and expending energy to preserve the few resources (e.g., students) that enable them to maintain the school. They use flexibility in their positions to redefine their roles, to provide services differentially, to expand certain roles, and to maintain their control over decision-making in crucial areas. They act as street-level bureaucrats, making on-the-spot policy interpretations to keep their schools functioning (Weatherley & Lipsky, 1977). Does it logically follow that assistants would want more flexibility? Or would more flexibility just increase ambiguity? Would they prefer, and feel more secure and satisfied with, explicit, clear, and constrained job descriptions?

One study found that effective central office supervisors are themselves highly flexible. They find the ambiguity, fragmentation, and invisibility of their roles to be useful for enhancing their ability to respond to individual differences, diversified staff, and constantly changing programs and staff (Floyd, 1987). Thus we see that at high levels of administration, flexibility, discretionary power, and ambiguity can be useful role characteristics.

An observational study found assistant principals exercising considerable discretion (Marshall 1985a). One urban assistant principal, who had 20 years experience in many schools, was described by teachers as the person who "holds this place together." She was observed creating her own interpretation of Public Law 94-142, bartering and negotiating to maintain a cadre of good substitutes, lobbying for program development, and overstepping her responsibility when she determined it was essential to prevent mounting problems.

An NASSP survey (Pellicer, et al., 1988) found that 50 percent of assistants felt they had considerable discretion although there was a decline in discretionary behavior since an earlier 1965 study. Thus discretionary power, flexibility, and/or strict definition of responsibilities will affect but not necessarily improve the satisfaction, functioning, and efficacy of the assistant principal.

However, now in the twenty-first century, the overarching effect of the federal NCLB legislation offers a staggering reduction of autonomy and flexibility in the administration of schools and districts. This is, of course, particularly true in those schools where "adequate yearly progress" is not occurring. In high-performing or non–Title I schools (in other words, wealthy schools), the loss of autonomy and flexibility is not a factor, but such schools are rare and decreasing across the face of public schools in this nation. As a result, junior administrators will have less autonomy today than at the time of the earlier studies, since there is less autonomy at all administrative levels. Those administrators who seek autonomy may look increasingly to nonpublic and charter schools where federal and even state intervention is reduced.

So What Does Give Satisfaction, Long-Term?

Recall the earlier description of research on career assistant principals in Chapter 3. That research, in addition to uncovering the ways these assistant principals shape their work and derive rewards, also found structures and supports that made their careers viable (Marshall, 1993). They included:

- Collaborative site team leadership;
- Being valued by the principal;
- Having the flexibility and time to develop pet projects for the school;
- Consistency in policies from above;
- Noninterference with their jobs;
- Policies supporting professional affiliations (paid trips to conferences, sabbaticals);
- Salary, benefits, and awards; and
- Being recognized as special.

Regarding recruitment and selection policies, some assistant principals preferred the traditional "good old boys" selection processes to today's assessment centers and certification exams. Similarly, there were increasingly technical assessments of their work. They worried that many of their tasks and ways of functioning will not be valued on checklists. In the same vein, the idea of internships and staff development seemed irrelevant to the progress of career assistant principals.

Policy actions that mattered included vacation policies and the freedom to actually get away without repercussions and piled-up work and protecting assistant principals from increased workloads that creep in with new programs, new students, new paperwork, and cuts in personnel. Finally, career assistant principals paid tribute to good school secretaries, guidance counselors, maintenance staff, and others as unsung heroes who keep schools calm.

Policy actions that disrupted their sense of well being included restructuring and site-based management that undercut their power and being required to do after-hours work for no pay, especially with no union protection. Undesirable policy pressures included the pressure to get doctorates, high turnover among higher level administrators, sexism, districts' preferences for "new blood" in administration, and lack of raises. Some would have liked to be called "associate principal," some wanted public perceptions changed so that their positions were not seen as career failures, and many would have liked their role definitions to provide more time in classrooms.

Beyond policies. Policies and programs seemed irrelevant to career assistant principals. When asked about support from the central office, most often the career assistant principal responds, as one said, "just give me room to work" (p. 42). What helped, instead, were things such as a sense of humor, "my Christian beliefs" (p. 42), and the variety of the job. They did value professional associations, especially the NASSP, for special programs for assistant principals, and they appreciated the efforts of local and state associations in promoting the value of the assistant principal position. As this reflection on the career assistant principal shows, the position can be shaped to be quite satisfying. Too bad it goes so unnoticed!

Progress in Valuing the Role

The old Austin and Brown (1970) study showed that principals recognize the value and importance of assistant principals more than assistants themselves do. An assistant principal may derive satisfaction from praise and from comments such as, "He holds this place together" (from a principal) or "She gave me the chance to do better in school" (from a student). However, the traditional way of assessing

Table 4.5   Salaries of School Administrators and Teachers

Superintendents	$125,609
Principals:	
Elementary school	$75,144
Junior high/middle school	$80,060
Senior high school	$86,160
Assistant principals:	
Elementary school	$62,213
Junior high/middle school	$66,360
Senior high school	$70,495
Classroom teacher	$45,646

the status, understanding, and valuing of a person, a position, and a role is by looking at the salaries paid.

The Educational Research Service compiles data that show the recent patterns in salary for educators, including assistant principals. Salaries of education administrators depend on several factors, including the location and enrollment level in the school or district. According to a survey of public schools (Educational Research Service, 2004), average salaries for principals and assistant principals in the 2003–2004 school year were as shown in Table 4.5.

As is seen, elementary assistant principals are paid less than middle school assistant principals. High school assistant principals receive the highest salaries among assistant principals. Interesting comparisons and patterns also can be seen. Principals are paid between $13,000 and $16,000 more than assistant principals. Of course, when comparisons are made with teacher salaries, one must recognize the difference between a nine-month and a 12-month contract. Detailed and recent data on regional and district-size differences for current assistant principal salaries are unavailable. However, based on anecdotal information and regional surveys of administrative salaries, the patterns of difference proportions are relatively stable.

Employment of education administrators is projected to grow faster than the average for all occupations through 2012 (www .collegrad.com). Nuanced data on assistant principals are hard to find. For assistant principal salary trends, we can draw inferences from recent salary data for secondary principals (Poppink & Shen, 2003): urban principals were paid more than suburban and much more than rural. On average, principals earned 63 percent more than teachers; their raises were slightly more than teachers' but slightly less than average workers'. There was tremendous variability across the states, and in contrast to national trends in women's earnings, female secondary principals earned higher salaries than males (probably because women teach longer before entering principalships). Principals' pay in nonpublic and charter schools was $12,000 to $16,000 less than public school principals' pay in these recent years. Finally, teachers perceived the higher pay for administrative positions as only a moderate incentive for becoming a principal.

These salary patterns reflect the tradition that rewards people who move up in a hierarchy away from children (leaving teaching, then moving from assistant principal to principal) and who move toward line positions, closer to district decision-making. They also reflect the tradition (long dispensed with in teacher pay schedules) that the functions performed in educating older students are more valuable or perhaps more difficult than those performed in elementary schools.

It is time to investigate below the surface of patterns reflected in administrator salaries. What are the dynamics affecting salary differences between men and women and between whites and people of color? Are there assumptions that tasks such as supervision of high school extracurricular activities are more valuable or difficult than supervision of elementary students or elementary school instructional leadership? It is time to examine pay and promotion patterns and raise questions about how different types of assistant principal roles are rewarded.

Some administrator associations are pressing for laws to allow "meet-and-discuss" negotiations for salary and benefits for assistant principals and principals. Such lobbying could be accompanied by action aimed at equalizing and improving the status, value, and pay of the assistant principal. School and societal values are reflected in administrator pay policies and in the amount of money allocated to support a program or policy. Therefore, whenever school districts assert new policies (e.g., for prevention, individualized instruction, or instructional leadership), questions should be raised about whether salaries and promotions in the district reward people for implementing such goals and policies. Demands for reform can be linked to questions about salary. Every new program taxes school administrators' time. Program proposals, therefore, should include designation of responsibility to person(s) and money set aside to buy their time. Policy analyses must calculate the human costs and recommend adequate resources. However, unfunded mandates, requirements, and demands are at an all-time high under the NCLB provisions, so budgeting for human costs is less likely than ever to occur.

OPENING UP THE REALM OF EMOTION AND MORAL PURPOSE

Long ago, organizational psychologists began to study motivation, satisfiers and dissatisfiers in the workplace, stress, and burnout. But those studies seemed to be used primarily to gauge how to heighten workers' productivity. Feminists must be given the credit for valuing the emotions of caring, connection, and relationship. Education scholars have begun to acknowledge that which has always been there, albeit pushed aside by administration sciences. Now, however, even business management has discovered "emotional intelligence."

We can make another leap forward by recognizing school administrators' stresses in work demands and in their personal lives. Speaking of principals, Grady (2004) lays out the array of roles, including listener, provider, cheerleader, team member, umpire, guardian, historian, and so on. She recommends taking time to sort, prioritize, and delegate rather than take on the stress of trying to fulfill all of these roles well.

Simply recognizing the personal and emotional aspects of administrators' lives will make a huge difference. "If educational reformers ignore the emotional dimensions of educational change, emotions and feelings will only re-enter the change process by the back door" (Hargreaves, 1997, pp. 108–109). Opportunities abound from this simple insight. As shown in Chapter 3, new research agendas are beginning to explore emotional work. Tapping into the emotional dimensions of the daily work and the original career motivations of the assistant principal is a great place to start rethinking the structure of their roles and, on a larger scale, the kinds of leadership we want in schools.

FACING FUNDAMENTAL DILEMMAS

To what extent are administrators, particularly assistant principals, able to examine different ways of filling administrator roles and alternative ways to make the system work? When faced with large societal problems, in the form of pregnant students, students whose special needs are considered low priority, or students with no understanding of English, how do administrators search for solutions? How well does the assistant principal cope with parents who see schools as places that help the middle class do well but only train the poor for continued poverty? How well can the administrator cope when explaining to students from poor families why the breakfast program no longer exists? Should the assistant principal suppress the ensuing conflicts when implementing innovations that are at odds with the standard curriculum? Have there been any attempts to rethink the fundamental assumptions of schooling to deal with these persistent societal and professional dilemmas? Have any popular books or movies recognized the assistant principal's value? Apparently not. The most dominant policies affecting schools (e.g., NCLB, school funding, teacher incentives) are primarily small changes, keeping constant the current assumptions about schooling. No radical rethinking has penetrated policy minds; therefore no major changes have penetrated to the work lives of assistant principals.

REFORMS

Reforms in the early and middle 1980s contained proposals for altering the education system that increased the responsibilities of assistant principals (and other educators) but decreased their control over decisions about what is important in the day-to-day functioning of schools and about long-term goals for schooling. National commission reports and the frenetic activity at the state level have generally led to demands for new policy implementation, with statewide testing, tougher curriculum, mandated homework, increased demand for monitoring instruction, and staff development. Throughout the 1980s, states increased centralization of authority, and state legislators, state boards, and governors heightened their interest in and control over schools. Statewide testing, for example, increased monitoring of district and site performance. Graduation tests and minimum competency tests, sometimes accompanied by demands for remediation programs, were popular policies that increased site administrators' responsibilities. District and school "report cards" make school-site performance highly visible. Many states and districts have increased their curriculum, testing, and remediation requirements.

As a response to these increased controls by the state, a shift to site-based management of schools flourished during the 1990s. These efforts were aimed at empowering teachers, but they did not reduce the state mandates for testing and accountability. The theory was that individual schools and classrooms that knew their students and communities best could successfully tailor teaching and programs to meet the mandated standards. Furthermore, administrators at all levels were to become facilitators rather than leaders. Intellectually, they were no longer the problem-solvers in some areas, since that responsibility was shifted to teachers. Ultimately, once a site-based decision was reached, administrators, especially assistant principals, assumed their roles of supervisors and inspectors, ensuring that teachers were following the directive the teachers themselves had agreed upon.

Beyond theory, in the realities of site-based management, in the best cases administrators and assistant principals were able to effect change in their buildings and be included in the local debates. Nonetheless, the consensus-building effort was time-consuming and frustrating for administrators who did much of the legwork, such as completing and documenting the new procedures and defending the school's practice to the central office and to parents and communities. The reform itself expected constant change and evaluation, which is stressful to schools even if they agree on the changes. In the worst cases, schools in one district had highly variable practices and materials, even textbooks, so that students transferring within the same district had to re-orient themselves to the new culture.

Attempting to sustain increased decision-making power and flexibility at the school site and "empowering" teachers to participate in that decision-making created new roles for administrators. Still another popular policy thrust, parental choice, places site administrators in a new competitive marketing mode. Such contrasting trends in policy leave assistant principals and principals in a flurry of contradictory activity. Proposals for restructuring schooling or rethinking the hierarchical control models of managing schools are not serious, as they seldom include the necessary time and resources.

Fundamental changes in assumptions, in modes of thinking and interacting, in professional norms, in professional and organizational culture, are not accomplished by fiat. Without the resources, educators will absorb reform thrusts as tiring alterations to the status quo. Assistant principals will still be expected to fill the maintenance and control functions, keeping students and teachers "in line." Teachers will not trust the administrators who, on the one hand, proffer entreaties for collegial decision-making with teachers and, on the other hand, closely monitor their compliance with the state model for good teaching and their ability to stay "on task" with the state curriculum and high test scores. Without clear, consistent, and holistic reform, no real change will happen in the education system. The old reforms of the 1980s and 1990s left assistant principals managing the same chronic fundamental dilemmas, with one difference. Reform thrusts left them accountable for increased productivity (student performance) with no increase in resources or time and with less flexibility.

The very popular business model that heralded a creative entrepreneurial administrative style in the 1980s and 1990s was a useful political ploy that anticipated NCLB. Political rhetoric promised that tightened controls and accountability would inspire competition and excellence. With the implementation of the NCLB legislation in 2002, all states were required to establish a standardized testing protocol. Students failing to make annual progress are required to receive additional academic services and interventions. Although these efforts look slightly different in all states, this was clearly a watershed moment in terms of reduced district/school autonomy and increased federal interference and control of the curriculum and the priorities of American education. In point of fact, this was a clear pendulum swing back from teacher empowerment and site-based management. Instead, schools are saddled with the most overwhelming ubiquitous federal bureaucracy ever imposed on local educational agencies and schools. Instead of focusing on the creative and exciting work of curriculum design and teaching methodologies matched to content, NCLB requires astute familiarity with statistics and data analysis. Assistant principals in today's schools must be well versed in item analysis, effective teaching, best practices, and evaluations tied to test scores. NCLB puts more money into teacher training as it reduces funds previously used for salaries and teaching positions. Assistant principals must know how to reach, motivate, and cajole teachers to use the federal monies for professional development in the narrowly focused areas of the state's curriculum and testing goals. Typically this means only mathematics and language arts.

All told, these trends take away site-level administrators' flexibility. Furthermore, they take away inducements (in the form of vocational education, sports, extracurricular activities, humanities, arts, and social programs) that have helped administrators and teachers deal with students and parents who are dissatisfied with the academic program. With Reagan's "New Federalism" of the 1980s, we saw the demise of federal categorical programs, which left many districts with fewer administrators and program specialists with special funding, but the student and parental needs and the expectations centered in those programs did not disappear. The reform effort of NCLB further narrowed opportunities, curriculum, and even course offerings for students as schools focus almost exclusively on the two standards, reading and math, required by the legislation and tied to funding.

Increased reforms leave assistants in new quandaries. Assistant principals, on the front line with students, faculty, and community members, cannot hide behind commission reports and clean new legislation. They must somehow explain to a parent when the categorical funds for a program are gone and certain children's special needs will not be met. They must also explain why the school has been labeled "failing" by the local media when it has received a state designation of "a school in need of improvement" based on annual progress of a particular subgroup. To make this manifest, imagine explaining to an auditorium of parents that the middle school has been designated to a second year of school improvement in math when math scores have gone up 6 percentage points per year for the last three years. Imagine further that the explanation is that a subgroup has failed to meet annual progress and thus led to the designation "in need of improvement." How does one explain that the underperforming group is special education students, which by definition would not make adequate yearly progress? These are the new challenges of reform for assistant principals in the twenty-first century. They face restricted autonomy and flexibility but are expected to communicate federal and state policies affecting the school that are not fully understood, even by the legislators who put the reforms in place.

Assistants must find ways to get teachers to cooperate on curriculum development and professional development when they are angry about the imposition of teacher accountability mechanisms. They must comply with, and support, new state policies that were devised without the involvement of the people who know the most about the issues at hand.

Assistant principals face these fundamental dilemmas daily. They may soon learn to filter them out of their consciousness so they can focus on getting the job done and on being evaluated as cooperative, loyal, and essential to the ongoing functioning of the system. That does not mean the fundamental problems have disappeared; it means assistant principals are being successfully socialized into the administrative culture.

Such conditions accentuate the continuing dilemmas of school administrators. Assistant principals see declining resources, declines in enrollment, a drop in public confidence in schools, aging faculties, continuous flight from public schooling, and lack of incentive to attract creative, inspired, and intelligent young people to educational careers (Boyd, 1983). They also witness an increasingly culturally, ethnically, and economically diverse student body being taught by an increasingly homogeneous instructional staff.

The assistant principal's voice needs to be heard as educators, policymakers, and citizens seek to define the problems in education. Assistant principals see them firsthand daily; they cope with the dilemmas of schooling—the dilemmas that cannot be solved by the current ways of thinking.

SUMMARY

This chapter has shown the areas of progress, the proposals, the programs, and the structures for affecting school administrators and for improving the assistant principalship. Some promising and useful projects are under way, but chronic problems remain.

It is important that those concerned with schooling and school administration have a sense of responsibility, involvement, and a guide to action for addressing the concerns of the assistant principalship.

The next chapter provides a range of proposals for change. Perhaps this book will serve as a call to action.

DISCUSSION QUESTIONS AND ACTIVITIES

1. Imagine that you are the State Superintendent or the Secretary of Education for the U.S. What changes would you make to certification requirements to support the plight of assistant principals in American schools?

2. Having reviewed the challenges and stressors in the assistant principal role, what is your plan to manage stress on the job? This answer will be highly individual but should be based on knowledge of yourself and your needs and interests and the stress you have experienced.

3. Talk to another assistant principal you know and interview him or her about the topics discussed here: loyalty, challenges, pleasures of the work, anticipated career steps in the next five years, etc. How does his or her perception compare to yours?

4. Identify indicators or vestiges of the three reform movements discussed in this chapter (Reagan Era—1980s, site-based management—1990s, and NCLB—2000s) in your current job. Discuss what these reforms look like today in your school or district and how they have changed since the time of their implementation.

5. Creativity in the job of assistant principal, sometimes referred to in this book as the behavior of the "street-level bureaucrat," seems to be not only a survival skill but a source of satisfaction. Look at your work as an assistant principal, and try to find examples of this kind of creativity or similar behaviors that advance goals without completely following the rules.

6. Describe your satisfiers in the job of assistant principal. Do you think there are more for assistant principals who have moved up from teaching at the same school, or less?

7. Design the ideal professional development for yourself as an assistant principal. Be specific about the topics, speakers, and format.

8. Good selection processes include a demonstration of skills by the candidates. Many schools now require teachers to do a demonstration lesson with students to showcase their skills. What would such a demonstration look like in an assistant principal search?

9. Describe equity in your school and district based on the gender and ethnicity of your administrators. What can you say to explain this diversity or the lack of it?

CHAPTER FIVE

A New and Different Assistant Principalship

I just want what most people want in their jobs—a little room to try out new things, decent pay, to be backed up by my boss when I try something, to get pats on the back when something I do works well, to have some control over what I do day to day, and to work with neat people in my profession.

—An anonymous, but typical,
assistant principal

All professionals want their work lives to have the following elements: flexibility, support, opportunities for satisfaction and job enhancement, a degree of control over the way to carry out the work, ways to get a sense that their work is valued, and affiliation with fellow professionals. Education professionals especially need to know that their hard work makes a difference for children and, through them, for a better world. How can the assistant principalship be improved so that individuals will experience these things? How can the problems in the assistant principal role be addressed?

Chapters 1, 2, and 3 have shown what we know about the position, and Chapter 4 identified areas of progress. Now, having established what we know, we proceed to recommend potential changes. This chapter is a search for possible improvements in the roles, training, selection, incentives, and recruitment of administration, and it shows the implications of reconceptualizing the assistant principalship.

The first section emphasizes small alterations in the current system. Such changes are often labeled "Band-Aids" to denote a "quick-fix" approach. Such suggestions do not question or change the current overarching structure; rather, they repair minor problems. Nevertheless, they offer useful and positive ways to enrich the work lives of assistants. The second section uses the assistant principalship as the impetus for a critical examination of schooling and offers suggestions for more radical change.

A word of caution: Before we can start altering job descriptions, training personnel, rewarding the instruction-minded, proposing scholarships for recruiting women and minorities, or suggesting any other strategy, we must remember the complex nature of the assistant principalship. Every set of understandings about who assistants are and what they do emerged from an evolving culture in school administration. Therefore, every change will reverberate through that culture, affecting the people and the work. For example, if school systems suddenly start selecting as assistant principals people who are excellent instructional leaders, who will assume the traditional assistant principal function of maintaining order in schools? Will such instruction-focused people ever have a chance for upward mobility if the principalship and superintendency continue to be positions in which political, financial, and crisis management skills are essential? What is an instructional leader, anyway? Should instructional leadership be an administrative function, or should we explore instead the possibility that teachers should take more leadership in instruction?

What if we decide that all assistant principals must get state certification through specific formal course work? Is that fair for those who live far away from universities? Will such a requirement exacerbate the shortage of administrative candidates? Should educators expand the responsibility of university professors and state bureaucrats and politicians in defining credentialing? Which course work should count: Does a course in math education count for administration? Does a district staff development workshop count? Should online courses from online universities count as much as the traditional immersion in university campus life for course work? Why do most administrative programs fail to offer a course in effective and efficient student discipline when all reports are that this is the crux of most assistant principals' work lives, especially at the secondary level?

Or suppose districts decide on strict definitions of assistant principal functions to reduce role ambiguity. How will this affect assistant principals who succeed wonderfully because of the flexibility to meet immediate needs in crises and who want to use the position as a place for experimenting and developing creative ideas?

Obviously, no single proposal for reconceptualizing the assistant principalship can address all possible anticipated and unanticipated consequences. A change in one part of a school system will affect the whole. The following proposals are ideas for discussion and experimentation, not guaranteed quick fixes.

SPECIFIC ALTERATIONS IN THE CURRENT SYSTEM

Many scholars and policymakers argue that tinkering with the system will achieve little improvement. However, there are specific alterations that would improve the lot of the assistant. (For more proposals and materials, see National Association of Secondary School Principals, 1987, 1991; Marshall, 1990; Porter, 1996).

Defining Roles, Tasks, and Functions

Even with efforts to describe the assistant principal's position, many districts see the role as the person to assist the principal in all administrative tasks. Some schools construct job descriptions (as mentioned in Chapter 2) for the assistant principal that are well specified and finely tailored to the particular school site. Schools with more than one assistant principal will often divide areas of responsibility, but even with such specification, the roles, tasks, and functions undergo constant informal negotiation. For example, when community drug programs are started, when state funds and mandates add programs or grants become available, new functions arise for the assistant principal. New tasks and new technologies also challenge current responsibilities. Suddenly, the assistant has the new job of managing computerized student accounting systems. Unanticipated crises such as teacher strikes, a principal's illness, and community protests over safety or sex education require school site administrators to forget job descriptions and pitch in. Principals and central office administrators, when faced with a task that they either cannot do or do not want to do, may assign the job to their assistants. Or principals may redesign job descriptions so that the assistant can have an opportunity to explore, develop, and test new areas of skill and expertise.

When assistants' roles are ambiguous, some important functions may be given short shrift. The assistant principal who has little sense of how to assertively take on an area of responsibility may never dare do more than wait for orders. He or she may never feel secure enough to do any long-range planning or develop innovative approaches to managing school problems. Without the ability to set priorities, without control over their time, assistant principals miss things that most professionals seek. The assistant principal whose job description seems to be "do everything the principal can't and doesn't want to face" will probably feel tremendous dissatisfaction with the position.

Whether or not schools provide them with clear job descriptions, assistant principals still may negotiate responsibilities and engage in activities that get the attention of superiors to enhance their chances for upward mobility. Role ambiguity benefits assistant principals who have support for being risk-takers, who have sponsors showing them how to see, grab, and succeed in areas that are district problems and challenges. For example, take a look at a very different, almost renegade assistant principal. Larry Cuban, who moved from teacher to "quasi-assistant principal" to superintendent to scholar, seemingly created his own role. He headed a program to train teachers within a site, negotiated with universities, and did managerial tasks for training teachers. He administered "by the seat of my pants," dealt with "nasty elbowing" politics, and took on extra duties to see that the project would continue. His principal was his "in-school boss" and the assistant superintendent was his other boss, who gave him a "long leash" as he dealt with visitors and courted opportunities for additional funds (1988, p. 86). Although he dealt with mundane tasks, he writes, "the frenzy of teaching, administering, and politicking exhilarated me" (p. 90). The contrast with the typical assistant principal role is startling! Such exhilarating role flexibility is not for everyone and perhaps not even good for a school site's needs, but it does offer insights about ways to provide excitement, creativity, and possibility for today's assistant principals. NASSP's efforts to include assistant principals on national-level committees (e.g., on NCLB and on Urban Education task forces) signify a major step in recognizing their insights into schools' needs. District- and state-level committees and task forces should do likewise, as a way of recognizing the value of the assistant principal.

Role negotiation. One possible way to provide the appropriate mix of stability and clarity of job expectations, while still providing challenge and opportunity for assistant principals, is semiannual role negotiation among the site administrators. If the assistant principals and the principals know that they will renegotiate job responsibilities on a regular basis, task assignments do not become a life sentence; moreover, assistant principals will be encouraged to propose exciting projects or new ways to approach difficult problems because they will experience a sense of professional autonomy. Assistant principals in charge of seventh grade discipline, who see that they cannot "prove themselves" unless they handle older students, might trade duties with another assistant principal. If assistant principals are saddled with all extracurricular and discipline duties one year, the negotiated understanding is that the next year they have a chance to implement their ideas for using curricular and academic activities to improve the school climate. Similarly, the principal who wants to expend time and energy on staff development may request that the assistant principals take on the burden of school-community relations.

This negotiation should be a formal process that occurs at set times each year in a retreat setting *away* from school demands. Informal role negotiation occurs naturally but informally, causing tension and competition among administrators. "Formal role negotiation" would bring this micropolitical process into the open. Assistant principals and the principal should have ample time to talk about their ideas, their role satisfactions, and their successes and failures in a relaxed, nonevaluative, and collegial manner, as fellow professionals in the administrative team. Such administrative team retreats, away from immediate crises and interruptions, would be symbols signifying the importance of administrative roles.

Job rotation. Similarly, administrative tasks and areas of responsibility may be rotated among the administrators according to an agreed-upon schedule. For example, the junior high assistants may rotate into the senior high after two years. This procedure should serve the same function as semiannual role negotiation, allowing variation, equal opportunity, and access to tasks that enhance visibility and widen experience. Moreover, like looping in elementary schools, it builds continuity with students as their assistant principal moves up to the high school with them.

However, not all tasks *should* be transferred. Most administrative tasks are continuous, never-completed responsibilities. In addition, administrators might avoid or limit special projects if they know their project will be rotated to someone else in six months. Job rotation, therefore, should be used if there is so much conflict and competition that role negotiation fails.

Specialization. A quite different approach would be to define assistant principal positions in detail for particular purposes and provide specific supports, expectations, and rewards for these specialists. A job opening can be advertised as "assistant principal for instruction" or "assistant principal for pupil personnel." Individuals seeking that job will know up-front their tasks, the criteria for judging their performance, their opportunity for interaction with superiors, their affiliations with other professionals, their future training and career chances, and what their daily work lives will be. They will shape their work around these clear realities. Similarly, the principal and the selection committee can be more certain about the qualifications expected and the kinds of support and guidance to give the specialist assistant principal. Such a specialist will have respect for a particular area of expertise and may be used as a district resource (e.g., for staff development and monitoring other such specialists).

Why not keep a districtwide list of all administrators' special expertise? Thus an assistant principal could be one of the district's official experts on computer programming, on Title IX, on the politics of PTOs, and so on. Every educator has some particular area of expertise that can be shared across the district and the profession. These are often unrecognized, untapped, and unrewarded, especially when the educator's primary responsibility lies elsewhere. School districts often fail to value the assistant principal who knows a great deal about a particular community-based or government program, about computers, about special education inclusion, about gender equity, and so on. There should be recognition for the assistant who knows the literature about stereotyping in the curriculum, the one who has experience in politics, the one who loves research and evaluation, or the one whose outside activities include lobbying for consumer rights or environmental protection. These people could be resources, special consultants to the school district.

This listing of all educators and their skill areas can be drawn on to meet needs as they arise. Superintendents, school boards, and principals—who need to appoint educators to lead task forces, to serve as liaisons with community groups, and to expand program offerings—can use this list.

Through this structure, an assistant principal who has hidden talents with computers could become head of the district computer advisory committee and a resource for the entire district. The assistant principal who knows how to eliminate sexism from the curriculum will now become the district's official liaison with the community groups that want sex equity.

From the list, educators (whether or not they have high visibility) have the opportunity to get official credit (a title, travel money, something to put on their resumes) for their contributions. In addition, the district benefits from a wide range of special expertise while at the same time providing educators with a sense that their talents are recognized and valued.

Titles. Why not call them associate principals? Why not create co-principalships? Symbolically, this would convey status and represent more accurately the roles played. These might be only token changes or substantial structural changes. But the changes might help in recruiting, recognizing, and retaining good educators who have to take on the array of general tasks that help the school. This would be a way to signify that the assistant principal role is not merely the "go-fer" for the principal.

Participatory Management

The traditional model of the management team is set up with the assumption that administrators manage and teachers do not. Successful implementation of management teamwork needs to be based on openness of communication and afterschool meetings for debriefing, thinking of the administrator's role as serving others, and giving credit to each person who contributes.

Increasingly, in management or team structures, decision-making, short- and long-range planning, and division of tasks are done with a teamwork approach, including the principal, assistant principals, department chairs, and teachers. Such an approach reduces the conflicts between teachers and administrators and among administrators.

However, participatory management requires that time be set aside for planning, that administrators and teachers be trained to share in the planning processes, and that administrators wipe out old assumptions about their need to keep everything under tight control.

Management team structures require assistant principals and other educators to learn to articulate their sense of what is needed. They might first have to *unlearn* the micropolitical and surreptitious ways devised for getting what they want and doing things their way that worked under a structure where they had little say in policymaking.

Affiliation-Support Groups

The assistant principal lives with the knowledge that daily work will include problems that are never solved, work that is never complete, joys that are never noticed, and needs that are seldom acknowledged. Everyone needs to share the joys and grouse about the problems with others who understand. The need for affiliation with peers may be met, but only haphazardly and intermittently, in casual social situations, in "Ben and Jerry days." An "in-group" mentality develops sometimes, providing affiliation and support for some but excluding others. Instead of haphazard affiliation for a few, assistant principals should create support groups that cross district lines and are open to all assistant principals (and interns working with them) to facilitate sharing of ideas, coping strategies, support, empathy, and networking and offer information on topics of current concern to assistant principals. This could be a grassroots organization or a subgroup of existing professional associations like the NASSP. It should, however, preserve the special function of addressing the particular concerns and needs of assistant principals and not be lumped with general administrative concerns. The Internet could be a great tool for national affiliation and support.

Sessions such as "How to Define Your Own Job and Still Get Along With Your Principal" or "Using the Curriculum for Discipline Management" as well as informal "gripe and brag" and "wine and whine" sessions would be particularly useful for groups of assistant principals and would give them a sense of affiliation with a group of supportive peers. Accessible, readable materials such as this book, the Phi Delta Kappan booklet, *The Role of the Assistant Principal* (Marshall, 1990), *New Voices in the Field* by Hartzell, Williams, and Nelson (1995), and also the new research presented in Chapter 3 can serve as discussion stimuli. The Peer-Assisted Leadership (PAL) Program is an example of year-long professional development aimed at reducing the isolation of site administrators as well as improving instructional leadership (Mueller & Lee, 1989).

Is This Relevant to You?

Have efforts to define roles and functions helped you?

What would prevent you from negotiating your roles? Does job rotation help or hurt you on the job?

Do you have a specialized skill that could be useful to the whole district?

How does associate principal sound? Co-principal?

Do you want more "say" in your management team decisions?

Who gets excluded from informal support groups, and what should you do about it?

Discretionary Power and Recognition

Many people chafe under the restrictions of being an "assistant" in hierarchical organizations, of constantly having to report, ask permission, plead for resources, and work according to someone else's plan. Teachers can close the door and, within accountability limits, do what they think is appropriate with their classes. But assistant principals often have no door to close and are often required to carry out procedures based on the judgments and values of others.

No amount of training or support will improve the assistant principalship unless there are some areas in their work lives where they have flexibility, independent resources, control, and the power to be the resident expert. These are basic needs for adult professionals.

When assistant principals push to move into higher positions, they are seeking increased autonomy and flexibility as well as status and money. Assistant principals, to help them persist in the daily challenges of their jobs, must have areas of discretion, authority, and autonomy. Special projects, start-up funds, titles, and management teams are possible structures for providing assistant principals with the opportunity to exercise their discretion and build areas of expertise contributing to the total operational success of the school.

Special projects. Suppose assistant principals' job descriptions included "developing and managing a special project that contributes creatively to the goals of the school or district." This would sanction them, allocate them time and resources, and challenge them to explore ideas of their own or borrow ideas from professional journals and conferences, to analyze school needs, to promote their idea, to create structures to implement it, and to have the sense of accomplishment from seeing outcomes from their own particular project.

While they would have the responsibility for building a rationale, promoting the project, getting people involved, obtaining the necessary resources, and managing the project, they would also get the satisfaction and sense of control and opportunity to run with their own ideas. They might find that this opportunity enhances their willingness to stay in the position, but some individuals may find that their projects increase their visibility and their desire to move into higher positions.

The special project would allow assistant principals to develop constructive projects and build independent administrative skills as a legitimate part of their job responsibilities, not as something that must be negotiated with the principal and relegated to the status of "something you can do after all of the real work is done." While such a project would not be the assistant principal's whole job (as with Larry Cuban above), it would provide the freedom for constructive creativity to blossom.

Start-up funds. Where possible, school districts can provide a fund of $600 for assistant principals to use as seed money for a special project. Guidelines should require that the money be used to develop something new that will contribute to the well being of the school.

Then assistant principals can, without further restrictions, use the money to write grant proposals, to take a course on computers in order to start a computer club, to attend a conference on educational research, to hire a consultant to help with interpersonal relations or community relations, or whatever *they* decide would help the school and their own functioning in it. The expense to the school district would be more than repaid in the good will, the new ideas, and possibly the reduced turnover and reduced dissatisfaction of incumbent assistant principals.

REASSESSING THE VALUE OF ASSISTANT PRINCIPALS

Why do so many assistant principals want to move up to higher positions? Higher salary, status, and power certainly serve as powerful incentives, making the position merely a stepping-stone to higher administrative positions. There are two problems arising from this use of the position: (a) Only a select few can move into higher positions, particularly in districts with declining enrollment, and (b) the assistant principal performs crucial functions in schools. Therefore, school districts need to find ways to support good people who *want* to stay in assistant principal positions and find career satisfaction there. This section explores several different ways to alter perceptions of the value of the assistant principal.

Promoting the Value of Assistant Principal Functions

To the person on the street, the assistant principal is the person who handles disruptive kids and does every unwanted administrative job. Many would probably characterize the assistant principal as an angry, frustrated person who is low on the totem pole of school hierarchies. This stereotype ignores the key functions served by assistant principals: holding the line on student control and picking up duties where the principal left off.

Few people recognize the efforts of assistant principals to expand their responsibilities and to make individual contributions to improving school programs and climate. No movie stars or television series bring the job to life and show the valiant efforts, the dilemmas, and the important issues faced by assistant principals. Few novels are written about educators generally, let alone about assistant principals. Television and movie portrayals of assistant principals are consistently unflattering. Yet every assistant principal has the sense that important elements in his or her school would disintegrate without an assistant principal's efforts.

A first step in improving assistant principals' and others' valuing of the position is exploring, defining, and disseminating information about their work. The position is unnoticed, unseen, concealed by school structure, and ignored in preparation programs. Lortie (1975), in *Schoolteacher*, wrote about teachers: what motivates them, what they are like, and what satisfies them in their jobs. Wolcott (1973), in *The Man in the Principal's Office*, showed the myriad functions of and demands on a typical principal. The superintendency has been studied a great deal. Now it is time to identify how assistant principals' work fits into the ongoing functioning of schooling, how assistant principals actually carry out their work, and what satisfies and frustrates them.

The studies reported in Chapter 3 begin this examination. In-depth research based on interviews and observations of a range of assistant principals can help educators and the general public move beyond their stereotyped views. Principals can read such works and be moved to alter school-site work arrangements. District, state, and university policymakers can draw implications about training, certification, salary, and career incentives.

Beyond research, the public and professional understanding of the assistant principalship can be facilitated by school districts and professional associations supporting workshops and presentations of innovative, workable practices in the assistant principal positions. There is a real need for inspired, research-based information telling the world about the ways in which assistant principals are essential to the ongoing work of schooling. In addition, these associations and districts, along with universities and state departments of education, should consider the special needs for training, self-renewal, and support of assistant principals.

Finally, it is important to examine whether the salary and status of assistant principals are sufficient for maintaining the integrity of the position. Are they enough to keep good practitioners satisfied with being there and devoting their full energies, loyalties, and expertise year after year? Or will they leave to go into real estate?

> ## Is This Relevant to You?
>
> How do you find ways to be autonomous?
>
> What pet projects do you nurture?
>
> If you had $600, what would be the best innovation to start in your school?
>
> When do you feel truly valued?
>
> If there were a popular book, movie, or television show about assistant principals what should be the themes?

PREPARATION, RECRUITMENT, AND SELECTION

A range of alternatives in the way assistant principals receive the right training (including inservice), learn to be leaders, and obtain their jobs can make quite a difference.

University and Professional Training

University programs for master's degrees, doctorates, and special certificates can be used to focus on the needs of assistant principals. The master's degree is the most logical place to focus on site-level administrators because most master's students aspire to or occupy those positions. This should be planned with the advice and involvement of education professional associations and should be aimed at integrating skill-building with knowledge. Training should not consist of simple recipes and checklists for managing administrative tasks because this will not fit all schools or emerging issues and problems. If, for example, a school district subscribes to the Madeline Hunter model of direct instruction, new assistants should know a great deal about that protocol with all of its strengths, weaknesses, and nuances. It is one thing to study theories of teaching and learning; it is quite another to use them as frameworks to confer with and evaluate classroom teachers.

Assistant principals, while learning skills through simulations, role-playing, and practice, should also learn from the literature on schooling about how their functioning fits into the bigger picture of school administration. For example, assistant principals may collect and analyze various discipline policies and procedures as an exercise aimed at widening their information base. Yet simultaneously, they should have readings and guided discussions that help them to see how discipline follows certain assumptions about the nature of students and about the role of schools in socializing children to be workers and orderly citizens. They should also examine how discipline instructs and assists with the broad management and climate of the school and its community. Similarly, as they listen to seasoned administrators describe their processes for handling school-community relations, aspiring administrators should read and discuss literature that helps them to see the political structure of education. In this manner, they can develop a leadership style. They can have awareness not only of past practices but also of a questioning search for a style that facilitates community, teacher, parent, and student participation. Discipline is an area that is woefully underdiscussed in graduate school. Due process is covered, but do new assistant principals really know when they abrogate it? Typically they understand the concept but do not recognize the practices that violate the right.

University and professional associations need to work as teams whose combined efforts can improve school administration. Universities and professional associations can have their strongest impact on aspiring potential administrators such as assistant principals. They can create appropriate training programs for people who are just beginning to form an orientation to the administrative role. They can have great impact on those who are actively searching for role models and workable strategies and can assist those who are searching for ways to manage the conflicts between professional and bureaucratic demands. By actively identifying, recruiting, and supporting individuals as they enter administrative positions, universities and professional associations can most strongly affect the way administrators define their roles and leadership styles.

This is also the best time to affect their competencies and their sense of professionalism as administrators. At this stage of professional development, future administrators may be more open to ideas about instructional leadership and to discussing the education system's perpetuation of racism, class bias, sexism, and poverty. Assistant principals can borrow from Grady's (2004) straightforward hints for principals to make time to be in classrooms and to set a high priority on supervision work. To begin their interventions for equity, they can use the strategies provided in Johnson's book addressing the achievement gap (2002).

At this stage, the aspiring administrator may be shocked at the overwhelming demands on administrators and may be searching desperately for management techniques. Before getting locked into a particular style of managing crises, making decisions, and setting priorities, the fledgling administrator can see, try out, and experience the value of various approaches to decision-making. Such administrators may be more likely to engage in participatory decision-making when appropriate or to expend efforts for more wide-ranging searches for solutions. They are more likely to forgo quick-fix solutions and to persist in getting schools to face fundamental dilemmas even though there may be no immediate solutions, measurable progress, or reward.

The balance of course work and practice is tricky. On the one hand, North Carolina's subsidized master's of school administration usefully combines university course work and internships that are often real assistant principal positions. Such an approach combines the special capacities of universities and of districts, state policy attention, and money. On the other hand, a university in Massachusetts turns out many administrative certificates for practitioners in Massachusetts and adjacent states. The program involves two intensive summer sessions and prolonged internships. The scholarship and teaching from the university are good, but the preparation is weak.

Finally, universities and professional associations can identify, recruit, train, place, and support women and minorities. This can work only if the groups devise continuous programs that prepare individuals for administrative careers or altering any old district practices that were exclusionary support groups. It does no good to put women and minorities through special programs with scholarships and then send them forth to cope in an environment where they will be excluded from informal communications and evaluated as less than competent when they display a leadership style that is different or do not conform to white male norms.

Sponsors, Role Models, and Mentors

Assistant principals who have sponsors or mentors greatly benefit from the specific advice, confidence-building, access to opportunity, and caring guidance. Some benefit from the visibility and a sense of belonging that comes from being a protégé of a powerful sponsor. But these relationships do not naturally develop for all aspiring administrators. People engage in mentoring and sponsoring when they see someone who they think has the potential to carry out a school administrative career very much like they did, thus continuing current practice and providing support and role models for a select few.

School districts could create sponsor-mentor banks, lists of experienced people who are part of a network of school administrators. These people would agree to be sources of career advice for aspiring administrators. Ideally, administrators should be able to draw from the resources in neighboring districts if regional sponsor-mentor banks could be coordinated, perhaps by a professional association, a state department of education, a county system, or a university.

All conferences and professional meetings should have specific times set aside when administrators can meet with those in the sponsor-mentor bank. To achieve the status of sponsor-mentor, persons must provide evidence that they have helped other administrators gain competence and move up in administration. They must prepare a statement for a directory of sponsor-mentors discussing particular areas of expertise and interest and displaying their mentoring credentials.

Particular preference should be given to individuals with the ability to think about how to shape the assistant principalship and how to develop potential leaders. They also should be individuals who can demonstrate that they have helped women and minorities attain administrative positions. They should be able to bridge the gap between universities and practitioners and, for example, help negotiate roles and assist in discussions for rethinking assumptions about administration.

Principals especially need to take seriously their responsibility to mentor their assistant principals. The old give-the-assistant-principal-the-jobs-you-don't-want model is not good enough. Principals' job descriptions should include recruiting and training new administrators. Doing so requires, at the very least, being thoughtful about formative evaluative feedback. It also means positioning assistant principals to enable them to have a wide range of tasks and a good view of, and visibility in, the district- and community-wide interactions encountered in senior leadership positions.

Internships

People usually have some image or stereotype of jobs as they make career decisions. They have vague ideas about what kind of people are "right" for the job, about what the challenges encountered and tasks performed in that job are. Based on that vague sense, they decide whether or not to leave their current position and take the steps required (extra training, job interviews, new tasks) to enter the new position. Much of this is based on incomplete information, and so it is risky.

Entering the assistant principalship means separating from teachers, seeking to be included with administrators, crossing a major career boundary to carry out very different tasks, affiliating with a different set of people, and managing major crises and dilemmas. Those who contemplate this move need to have a period of reality testing. Internships would allow them to follow several assistant principals through a workweek in several schools, watching and questioning the meaning of the behavior, words, and interactions of administrators.

The internship should be guided by a university program or a professional association. Aspirants should be engaged in questions about the function of administration and about their own fit (emotionally, intellectually) with the job. Internships should be "dressing rooms" where aspirants see if the role is comfortable and satisfying. Interns should get advice about the sorts of training and alterations that would be required to make them fit and the degree to which the aspirant can shape the position. Interns should be exposed to the satisfactions, frustrations, and conflicts in the position. The purpose of internships is immersion in reality—getting beyond the stereotype.

The internship should be deemed successful if the person forges ahead for a shining career in administration. It also should be deemed successful if an intern, upon seeing the tasks and dilemmas of administration, concludes that he or she prefers to stay in the classroom. Sometimes one emerges from the dressing room with clear knowledge that the outfit is just right. Just as often, the verdict is "Just right for someone, but not for me!"

Recruitment and Selection

Chapter 2 described typical ways in which assistant principals recruit themselves or get encouragement, apply for positions, and go through selection processes for assistant principal positions. Assuming that districts want to promote the most able, intelligent, and creative people for administrative positions, there are ways to improve recruitment and selection. Schools will benefit if the pool of administrative applicants is widened, if the career is attractive to more people, and if the process for selecting and promoting administrators is fine-tuned.

First, education systems must send out a message that the administration career *truly wants* people who are women, who are ethnic minorities, and who in other ways differ from the current stereotype of administrators. Statements like "we are equal opportunity employers" will not be believed until educators see evidence that administrators support and value people who are different. Anyone can see that tokenism will not work; tokens are people who are alone, without support, and excluded from the crucial informal network of communication among administrators. Without changes, schooling will suffer as competent women and minorities move away from education into careers with more equal access.

In a time in this country when controversy over same-sex unions and benefits is at the forefront, school districts should also open their thinking to include members of the gay and lesbian community in the field of administration. Just as issues for minority students have been raised for policy attention, issues for gay and lesbian students must be understood, leading to changes in policies and programs. Seeing responsible role models builds futures for all students. Those of us who have worked in education for decades know well that some of our best teachers are gay, and when they are selected as administrators they too can bring a new perspective to the work. The very same anxiety that surfaced two decades ago about African American administrators now quietly serves to disqualify good candidates in this group. Will they be too assertive or outspoken for the rights of gay and lesbian students? Will they be unaccepted by parents, other administrators, and the community at large?

Specific proposals include the following: (a) Pay women, ethnic minorities, and people with different career experiences to speak to student teachers and teacher groups and to serve as role models and career advisers. (b) Provide scholarships and internships particularly for underrepresented groups. (c) Require the state department of education to employ persons whose specific responsibility is training school boards and administrators to identify the barriers to

women, gays and lesbians, and ethnic minorities entering administrative careers and to create district-specific structures to recruit and
support their successful advancement. These persons would also
monitor districts' assertions about being equal opportunity employers. No district should be allowed to publish this assertion until filing proof of hiring, training, support, salaries, selection policies, and
results in terms of rapid progress toward equity in numbers of underrepresented groups in administrative positions. (d) Disseminate
(through conferences, educators' journals, and department of education directives) information about employee rights to encourage
school districts to equalize access for gays and lesbians, women, and
ethnic minorities to administrative careers.

Second, assistant principalship vacancies should be advertised
widely. Often principalships and higher positions are widely advertised but announcements of assistant principal vacancies are kept
within districts. Very few positions are advertised across state lines.
As a result, administration is inbred; educators who wish to enter
administrative careers must wait for someone to die or retire in their
own districts, especially if they have no sponsorship. State departments of education or professional associations should maintain
computer banks of available positions and provide information about
administrative openings to interested educators from any state.

Third, selection committees should not expect applicants to be
familiar with the politics of a particular district. An administrator
must, of course, have the sensitivity and ability to function in the
midst of conflicts in values. Too often, the person who gets through
the selection process is the one known to be on the same side of a
current controversy as the majority of the people on the selection
committee—that is, a person who is an insider. This bias in the
process creates a kind of "groupthink," an administrative culture in
which no creative ideas are spawned and conflict is suppressed
rather than addressed. Individuals with administrative potential from
opposing camps or from other districts will not advance.

When assessment centers are used, they should be free, provided
by teacher and professional associations in inservices, or used as
training tools in universities. They should be focused on assessing
the competencies of individuals in the areas that the job requires and
adapted for the selection of assistant principals. Beyond this, additional revisions of the assessment center approach should incorporate evaluations of aspiring leaders' ability and propensity to be

innovative and to enact alternative approaches to leadership. "Same-old" is not good enough.

Fourth, districts should invest time, money, and personnel in selecting assistant principals. The assistant principal of today may be the superintendent of tomorrow. Too often, the assistant principal is selected without a search for options, consideration of possible redefinitions of the position, assessment of needs, or consultation with many of the people who will be affected by the assistant principal. Frequently the principal, without time or resources to invest in the selection process, chooses the person whose main qualification is a recommendation through the administrator grapevine, who is adequate but perhaps not the best candidate available.

Certification

Altering certification policies is one of the main mechanisms whereby state-level policymakers affect education in all school districts. In many states, the requirements for administrative certification are decided by a commission that invites the involvement of professional associations, universities, and citizens as well as state departments of education and legislative officials. Serious proposals for altering the training and minimum requirements for administrative certification, if passed, can alter the composition of the administrative ranks. For example, states could require all administrators to serve in internships; pass competency tests; and/or take courses on instructional management, children with disabilities, racism and sexism in education, and computer applications for administration.

No changes should be implemented without considering spin-off effects, because changes in certification can affect an entire state. For example, requiring more course work might exclude individuals with family responsibilities, especially when universities are distant. Raising standards through a written test may exclude some people who can perform well in many of the assistant principal functions but do not do well on written assessments. Moreover, in an already shallow applicant pool, certification requirements that appear to be barriers will be counterproductive. However, if aspiring administrators saw the elements of certification as tightly joined to the job, they might be much more agreeable to change, which will be a part of any revision to certification. Care must be taken so that valuable elements are not lost in the change process. Putting more responsibility in universities, in local districts, or in professional associations will decrease the sense of legitimacy and the standardization that comes from state certification. And decreasing the involvement of professional associations, local practicing administrators, or universities would risk losing the particular knowledge bases, authority, and expertise of each group. All must be involved, but no one group should dominate the training and selection process.

Thus the participants in policymaking for certification should continue to be the (sometimes tenuous) partnership of state departments of education, education professional associations, and university professors. However, they should first pay attention to the assistant principalship and analyze the requirements for the role, thinking of the position as the place where educational leaders begin their administrative careers. They should then propose alterations that will strengthen the training and redirect the orientation of assistant principals. In their planning, they should also create procedures and learning experiences so that these administrative candidates know how to address the concerns of all citizen groups (including those who are critical of school systems and their administrators). Learning should include ways to address inequities and to empower teachers in "restructured" schools.

Certification processes should be structured so that the result is certified administrators who constantly strive for improvements in instruction, who lead schools to work well with the community, and who support educator teams to work together to address fundamental problems such as low resources, inequity, inappropriate policies, unexamined achievement data, and inadequate support while continuing to serve as the individuals who maintain the stability of the school and its climate.

STAFF DEVELOPMENT, WORKSHOPS, CELEBRATIONS, AND SPECIAL CONFERENCES

Celebrating assistants and giving attention to their special needs can occur in retreats and statewide or regional conferences or workshops. Administrators' associations could recruit new members by addressing assistants' special needs. State departments of education and university programs can offer one- to two-day workshops or one- to two-week academies. Foundations can subsidize such efforts.

The assistant principal frequently takes on myriad tasks without formal training and without anyone to help. This stressful sink-or-swim approach works for assistant principals who have support from understanding families and guidance from sponsors and mentors. What appears to be survival of the fittest is actually survival of the ones who find informal training and support.

Assistant principals need training and support to enable them to manage tasks and responsibilities such as discipline, scheduling, and extracurricular activities. (Downing, 1983, offers "skill-builder" exercises.) But beyond this, assistant principals need to be prepared to fill the roles and functions of administrators and to face the fundamental dilemmas in administration as described in the previous chapters.

Assistant principal academies could fill some gaps. The most efficient approach would combine the needs and resources of a county or region for a one- to two-week summer experience. But a three-day summer retreat, assisted by consultants and continued by district support and study groups, can serve specific district purposes. One such experience (described in Peterson, Marshall, & Grier, 1987) was designed to fill a superintendent's agenda to recruit "a new breed" of administrator. Assistant principal academies, created with the shared expertise of practicing administrators and professors, would highlight assistants' special needs and provide them with skills and career decision-making experiences (Peterson, et al., 1987). On a smaller, more economical scale, the one- to two-day conferences mentioned in Chapter 4 are a good start.

Important elements include (a) bringing elementary, middle, and high school administrators together sometimes, while providing job-alike times for discussion of their level-specific issues, (b) convening at a pleasant location with a good hotel and receptions to convey honor, status, relaxation, and special treatment, (c) creating a "job bank," (d) creating a state-level awards program for the assistant principal of the year and publicity to create role models and convey status, and (e) finding opportunities to place assistants on critical committees (district, regional, state, and national). This approach is difficult because assistants do not control budgets and because they are usually required to stay at the school site to enable the principal to go to conferences.

With improvements in training and support, the assistant principalship can be altered to be less stressful, and those who fill the job can be more skilled, creative, and able to work on long-range planning. At a time when teacher induction is touted everywhere as a means of training and retaining staff, there is almost no talk of such programs for new administrators in the literature or in practice. Nonetheless, the stability of the school's administrative team is critical, especially as public education faces some of the most dramatic retirement figures in the last 50 years.

Is This Relevant to You?

What will you do to ensure that assistant principal training is task-relevant?

How can you increase inclusiveness in mentoring?

Could you really back out if you found you disliked administration?

What will you do to eliminate subtle exclusions of women and minorities?

Which elements of the licensure process are most essential to certify good administrators?

How can you create celebrations and conferences for assistant principals?

A DEEPER CUT: CHANGING PROFESSIONAL AND CULTURAL ASSUMPTIONS

Read this new-sounding description of the Michigan Assistant Principal of the Year for 2004–2005, who was an educator for 30 years: "Mr. Matthews . . . epitomizes the concept of servant leadership . . . he has redefined the perception of the role . . . from that of a stern, authoritative disciplinarian to one of a caring, compassionate student advocate who assists them in realizing and dealing with the consequences of their choices" (http://www.meemic.com/commasyr CKR.htm, 2005). Sounds like we're ready for reconceptualizations.

Reconceptualizing Assumptions About Administration

No substantial change will occur in the deeper culture of the profession of leadership or in the societal assumptions and expectations for leaders and for schooling with mere quick fixes. Deeper and wider searching and critique is needed. The assistant principalship is a fine place for initiating such reconceptualizing and critique. As the entry-level position within which assistant principals are socialized for leadership, the position *can* be re-visioned so that incoming leaders structure their tasks for leading schools and their orientation to the functions of school leadership differently. Yes, assistant principals are vulnerable, but as new leaders are in great demand, they are also powerful. This section proposes the kind of critique and reconceptualizations for such deeper and wider searching.

Even with opportunities for rotating and altering the tasks of assistant principals, many will view the position as undesirable and will continue to leave it for higher pay and status. And women and minorities will continue to see the evidence of their unequal access. Tinkering with structure can help in small ways. However, assumptions about the administrative structure, leadership, and the fundamental purposes of schooling need to be examined and challenged to retain good educators who are excited about taking on leadership jobs. This section cuts deeper; it proposes alterations that delve into the cultural and political assumptions about the purpose of schooling. It offers more radical ideas that challenge the way we generally think about administration, with important implications for assistant principals.

Shifting Dominant Views of Schooling

In their positions of vulnerability, we cannot expect assistant principals to be different unless societal expectations for leaders are shifted to embrace new styles.

New metaphors for leaders. A cursory examination of educational administration textbooks shows that most illustrations are line and staff charts of hierarchies in schools. Such is the graphic image used to train educational leaders. Models, pictures, and metaphors are lenses for understanding and challenging assumptions about leadership in administration and the structure of schools.

Long ago, Schein (1985) proposed that good leaders are culture managers, presenting a very different model or metaphor for educational administration. But people organize their work according to the images, ideas, or metaphors that they use to conceptualize their jobs. The dominant management metaphors are managing as a machine, an organism, a marketplace, and a conversation (Mitchell, 1983). The first two, machine and organism, are built upon a hierarchy. But these two metaphors do not fit principals: schools are not neat hierarchies. Nor does the marketplace metaphor fit, although it has dominated education policy development and central office administrators, linking explicit goals and rewards for specific performance.

The fourth metaphor, managing conversations, originates from an affective bond between organizational participants and is based on their shared meanings embodied in a common language. This metaphor imagines management's function to articulate common purposes and motivate individuals to cooperate in carrying out those purposes. Too often, principals neglect this metaphor and thus fail to encourage organizational participants to share in the cultural meaning-making within the organization. Yet this is where most of the work of assistants occurs.

How well do we prepare, support, reward, and promote administrators in this practice of building cultural meaning and communicating common purpose? Symbolic leadership (Bolman & Deal, 1984; Meyer & Rowan, 1978) helps an organization's participants (janitors, students, parents, teachers, and so on) coalesce around common ideas about purpose. Stories, ceremonies, heroes, and heroines are elements of the organizational culture. Symbolic leadership incorporates an understanding and appreciation of these cultural forces. Assistant principals need to learn this in their formal and informal training. Staff development, university courses, and internships should incorporate literature and experiences to develop appreciation of leadership through conversations, through collaborative meaning-making. Such instruction is not enough, however. Fledgling administrators need to see symbolic leadership modeled. Most important, they need to value symbolic leadership as an interaction that incorporates the full range of (often conflicting) goals of the varied participants and *not* as a method for using cultural tools to manipulate people.

Analysis of metaphors and the language of current administrators is a promising way to uncover the latent values and perceptions of those who manage our schools (Bredeson, 1988; Marshall, 1988).

Assistant principals need to understand the importance of culture, and they need to identify the ways their values (and their metaphors and language) guide their behavior. With such understandings, they would be more self-reflective and capable of working within the organizational culture.

Restructuring hierarchies. Educational administration hierarchies assume that people in higher positions are more important, more worthy of high pay, more correct in their judgments about what policies will work, and better able to decide how to alter the work. This structure is an adaptation of management and behavioral sciences, based on assumptions that the major concerns of administrators are control, maintenance of efficiency, and engineered change. Such assumptions ignore the social and cultural goals of education. They cut off the possibility of cultivating a "climate of professional dedication" among those who work in schools. They also demean the professional sense of people who are *closest* to the actual work of the schools, managing instruction, by placing them at the bottom of the hierarchy. They exacerbate the tension that assistant principals experience working between teachers and higher-level administrators.

However, theorists and practitioners have promoted the importance of including the people who implement policies in decision-making. As early as 1926, Mary Parker Follett (p. 33) asserted that to get things done well, one should "unite all concerned in a study of the situation" for decision-making rather than simply giving orders from on high. Many have proposed various devices such as the management team approach and quality circles. These ideas are promising but require a change in assumptions about status and leadership.

Current restructuring efforts do not always embrace such changes. In some cases, people at the bottom of the hierarchy may see restructuring proposals as simply another manipulative device to obtain cooperation, leaving them with the major implementation work and no new status, resources, or rewards for their efforts. The ways of thinking about and responding to decision-making will not change while the hierarchy remains intact. They will not change without challenging the assumption that people in higher positions know best and should have more power, status, pay, and final authority.

Real restructuring seldom occurs, since societal assumptions about top-down leadership are so culturally embedded and reinforced in assistant principals' training and internships. Also, attempts such as site-based management and collaborative teaming are undermined by policy pressures that tighten accountability for results.

Real restructuring will occur only with shifts in the prevailing definitions, metaphors, and assumptions that are the basis of what we call leadership, administration, and the structure of schools. It could even include schools that eliminated administrators and had lead teachers. Some of these reconceptualizations are being discussed in literature on educational leadership but too often as merely interesting theoretical challenges. Some are quite radical changes, with very different metaphors and images of leadership. But they are worth discussion as new ways of framing the professional socialization of new leaders, starting with the entry-level position of the assistant principal.

No assistant principal can change the professional culture alone, however. To do so would be such a career risk, such defiance of dominant values, that he or she would be a career martyr. Still, assistant principals and their colleagues can ponder the possibilities from provocative insights for envisioning a new professional culture that are presented in the next section.

Is This Relevant To You?

Who among school board, central office, or site administrators would like to talk about alternative leadership models?

Where have you seen evidence of softening of hierarchies?

What would be the risks in your enacting different leadership styles?

ALTERNATIVE LEADERSHIP THEORIES AND MODELS

The dominant bureaucratic model for leadership—in which leaders are like CEOs, managing for efficient production—has not worked for schools. An array of alternative models and theories exist in the newest literatures on school administration. They could radically alter the recruitment, retention, and satisfaction as well as the overall effectiveness of school leaders. We offer them here for consideration, as they might trickle down to the assistant principal.

Transformative Leadership

A new model of leadership (and not the rational science of administration) has been proposed and named. According to Burns (1978), organizations need "transformative leaders" whose purposes and values are authentic and well articulated. Leaders should be "transformative intellectuals" (Giroux, 1988) or "critical humanists" (Foster, 1986) who constantly reflect on how the organization is working to expand human potential and transform society to eradicate racism, classism, and sexism. Instead of learning how to manage and control community unrest, teacher insubordination, student dropout rates, or "uppity" women, such leaders would engage in a continuous quest to examine the root causes of such dissatisfaction and alter the organizational arrangements that hurt people's opportunities.

Leaders as Critical Humanists

Management, rational systems, and bureaucratic theories have guided the training of administrators and the structuring of schooling. According to these theories, problems can be fixed by managers' time-and-motion studies; planning, programming, budgeting, and execution; management by objectives; or the latest proposed stratagem. Unfortunately, NCLB has added significant credence to this long-held and simplistic notion of fixing educational problems. However, scholars and those interested in changing the plight of assistant principals and enabling them to meet enormous changes in and the tremendous needs of the current school-age population can learn from the challenges of critical theories.

Critical theorists pose an upsetting challenge. Tracing the historical development of institutions, they demonstrate the ways in which schools assist dominant power elites by suppressing the expression and aspirations of the poor and powerless and training a class of workers to comply with workplace routines. The factory model, with time-clocked units (Carnegie units or seat time requirements) of learning, division of labor (e.g., subject area teachers and administrative specialists), and attempts to standardize parts (e.g., children), was built into the structure of schools. Schooling became the answer to the challenge of "the unwashed hordes" of immigrants in the late 1800s and early 1900s; schools could transform this immense variety of new Americans into a homogenized whole through political socialization in the curriculum (e.g., American history) and the "hidden curriculum" (e.g., sex-role socialization and traditional American family values).

But critical theorists' challenges are not merely historical exercises; they demand an examination to discover how schools continue the practices of sorting and homogenizing and how schools continue to work for the benefit of dominant power groups, actually functioning to disadvantage the already disadvantaged. These critiques—coupled with minorities' unequal access to the benefits of schooling, young people committing suicide, children bearing children, women gaining doctorates but not jobs in educational administration, and high superintendent turnover—leave scholars and critics questioning the fundamental assumptions undergirding educational administration.

Realizing that organizations are "social constructions of reality" empowers people to create their own meaning and purpose for their organization (Berger & Luckmann, 1967; Greenfield, 1986). Leaders' roles, then, are to coordinate symbols and ceremonies as well as resources and tasks to support the collective meaning-making. If organizations and norms for good leadership are socially constructed, made up by collective powerful minds, then they can be deconstructed and reconstructed by powerful minds. Leadership and administration, then, are no longer seen as apolitical rational/technical operations set in stone; instead, an interactive process constructs them. Leaders do take political, values-based stances aimed at directing schools toward achieving goals. Leaders' value stances, therefore, are more important foci than their technical expertise with budgets and buses.

Models for administration that acknowledge responsibility, right judgment, and reflection as legitimately and inevitably part of administrative action emphasize the value bases of leadership and open up a discussion about the values, morals, delights, and rages that energize educators. Therefore they encompass the passion that drives an assistant principal to go the extra mile for a kid or a group of parents. They encompass the ideals of educators whose career choice was motivated by a desire to make a better world. And they encompass the anger of the assistant principal who encounters professional shock in seeing waste, inequitable treatment, stupidity, and so on, who feels the "moral outrage in education" that is so often repressed (Purpel, 1999). Thus the human and moral element of leadership can be coupled with the critical theorists, as in William Foster's view of critical humanist leaders (Foster, 1986).

Critical humanist leadership encompasses the critical theorists' insights about institutionalized inequities. Critical humanist leaders, however, feel empowered in their ability to construct new realities for schools and for leadership. Their leadership, then, is a constant search for improvement of the human condition through their work in schools. Their daily task decisions are anchored in the vision of a moral order in which justice, equality, and individual freedom are uncompromised by tradition, compromise, or the needs of elites (Prunty, 1984). Such a leader must be adept in the political world to be effective and to provide methods for the oppressed to gain power, while viewing school policy critically to expose oppressive structures.

What does this mean for assistant principals? They must reflect on their actions. They must consider whether their detentions, their parent conferences, and their interactions with new teachers will empower and democratize or whether they will dispense goods to the "have-nots" as much as they consider traditional questions such as whether their action is decisive, quick, and efficient. They must constantly survey their organization, searching for patterns and incidents in which societal inequities are played out in schools; and they must constantly find ways to alter those patterns to prevent those incidents. Such leadership is ultimately aimed toward wholesale reconstruction of political institutions and public life.

Intentional Leadership

In contrast to the bureaucratic model, Wissler and Ortiz (1988) posed the idea of "intentional leadership," in which the leader starts with a vision that will give structure to the process and help to resolve potential problems associated with the envisioned change. The intentional leader holds certain beliefs regarding people and the way they function in organizations—beliefs in their strengths and powers, which can be released if individuals are given room, faith, and trust to exert their power and capabilities (Wissler, 1984). The intentional leader defines the framework, provides the resources, does the monitoring, and makes it possible for people to function in such a manner. In intentional leadership, the organization's members work together on a "project" that actualizes the organization's values. The leader's function is to make choices that improve the human condition through the use of the organization and to coordinate work on the project. The organization is an instrument for releasing the power for good in individuals.

This model is quite different from the models in which maintenance of bureaucratic rules and controls predominate. Such a model is more appropriate for the administration of a sociocultural organization like a school (Clark & Meloy, 1988).

These ideas require reconceptualizing school administration so that senior administrators are viewed as coordinators of services and resources, servants of those who do the work of instruction. The valued positions would be those closest to instruction. Teachers and the administrators who work most directly in support of instruction would have the highest value, status, and pay. Such a reconceptualization would require radical change not only in the thinking but also in the structures of school organizations. The assistant principalship is the ideal position in which to try such restructuring.

Management team structures come closest to implementing intentional leadership when they involve all educators in defining problems and creating solutions. The assistant principalship, viewed as a training ground for intentional leaders, would be a valuable, desirable position for facilitating instruction and coordinating resources as part of the management team.

Substantial structural alterations would be required to reconceptualize the educational system's hierarchy so that administrators are viewed as coordinators and administrators and teachers work as teams. School administrators would have to question the value of hierarchical control. Those in power in the hierarchy would have to consider sharing that power. The first step would be in redefining the assistant principalship, the training ground for education leaders.

Feminist Perspectives on Leadership

Reforms of schooling have ignored feminist insights and have failed to challenge male-dominated conceptions of educational purpose, of students, of teachers, of curricula, of pedagogy, and of the profession of education. Feminist and critical theories offer lenses for looking at schools and understanding how the social construction of gender—how confining constructions of masculinity and femininity and classifications according to race/ethnicity, class, and sexual preference—limit human possibilities. Policies such as affirmative action and the Equal Rights Amendment come from liberal feminism. Such laws assume that simply eliminating barriers and placing women in positions will change institutional and cultural values. For assistant principals and for leadership, this only means that women would have the opportunity to become like white male leaders.

But further feminist scholarship demands examination of intimate relationships, values, and power arrangements. "Women's ways" feminism asserts that women have a different socialization, developing different orientations to moral decision-making, ways of knowing, and ethics (Gilligan, 1982; Noddings, 1984; Belenky, et al., 1986). These perspectives value women's subjective experience. They offer hopeful new visions of relationship and community-building, of networks of caring and nurturance; they challenge men and women to value the emotions and tasks usually designated as women's work for the private sphere (e.g., child rearing and caregiving).

Promising alternatives are generated from women's ways, such as the possibility of facilitative, nonhierarchical leadership—power-with rather than power-over—and coalitions built from women's commonalities, such as the women's movement to save their children from war and ecological disasters (Elshtain, 1997). However, women's ways, pursued without recognizing how these are devalued and relegated to the private sphere, leave women vulnerable and segregated with all the caring and community duties and no recognition of the political forces defining their worth. Furthermore, this view seems to endow all women and no men with these perspectives on relationships and caring.

Power and politics feminism helps explain informal politics, such as when men get credit for women's ideas and when women are supposed to defer to men. In turn, it helps explain the power behind the political decisions establishing the managerial model for school leadership (Tyack and Hansot, 1982) and a coinciding gender hierarchy, reified and perpetuated by sponsorship and by the fact that, by controlling the definitions of good leadership and policy, white male elites can squelch challengers. Thus "dominance is maintained, and the actions of the powerful are seen as virtuous, valued actions" (Ortiz and Marshall, 1988, p. 136).

Power and politics feminism incorporates the intertwining of sexuality and politics. For assistant principals, this highlights the power and dominance issues in bullying and sexual harassment in schools. It reveals the sexual politics of men's domination of conversations and meetings. It calls for assistant principals to direct special attention to the power of informal curricular messages that pressure girls into fixations on pleasing boys and being thin, and boys into feeling that drama club and art are not as valuable as football. It requires assistant principals to constantly monitor, for example, computers, maths, sciences, athletics, career counseling, and curriculum materials to prevent schools from sending life-limiting stereotyping messages.

The feminist critique asserts (a) that leadership and organization theories are the brainchildren of male scholars looking primarily at the leaders and the workings in male-dominated and male-normed organizations (Shakeshaft, 1987) and (b) that bureaucracies function to discredit and exclude those who raise uncomfortable questions and defy the norms, thus excluding women and minorities and reinforcing the power of the elite (Ferguson, 1984). Such a critique does help explain the continuing underrepresentation of women in leadership roles. Marshall and Mitchell (1989) demonstrated how this feminist critique helps explain the experiences of female assistant principals. (In a later section we recommend "Looking at Equity Through Cultural and Political Lenses" to expand and deepen women's issues in leadership.) The deeper question remains: How can women see and articulate the injustices of a system structured in the masculine?

Is This Relevant to You?

Have you tried any aspects of transformative or intentional leadership?

How could you get your community to understand and support critical humanist leadership?

What should a man learn from reading and seeing feminist leadership?

Why would female leaders take on more typically male-stereotyped behaviors?

Emotionally Engaged, Relational, and Caring Leadership

Current professional patterns seem to require administrators to detach their personal and emotional senses and, instead, guide their work choices by policy, rules, and tradition. These well-intentioned patterns, derived from bureaucratic assumptions, aim to ensure fairness, equity, and consistency in school workplaces. They guard clientele against whimsy, biases, and unpredictability, and they help people know what to expect.

As with many well-intentioned policies, these have unintended negative side effects. First, most educators' original career inspiration emanated from ideals and desires, and the same feelings and motivations are often the source of their willingness to "hang in there" in spite of angry clientele and low salaries. Educators' career passions often come from a desire to "do good" and nurture and help young children, improve society, and especially to help the less advantaged, to contribute to empowerment, to support children's excitement about learning, and even to build a democratic society.

Yet school administration, indeed all professional socialization for educators, treats such emotion and idealism as personal and as belonging to the private sphere. Indeed, administrators are often told—and then tell others—not to take things personally. They learn to avoid the angst-ridden moral dilemmas, the feelings of shock and anger at system shortcomings, and even exuberant expressions of joy or love. Passions, fury, excitability, special preferences, family worries—all are personal and inappropriate, to be wiped clean from the professional educator's demeanor and kept separate from decision-making. Inconvenient, messy, and bothersome issues that complicate the main public mission are pushed aside. Issues centering on loving, caring, and relationship, on insights from one's personal life, gender, and sexuality are not to be presented. Complicated personnel issues like depression and low morale, family needs, and the like are thrown into a huge category and labeled "personal" and, therefore, dealt with as individual problems, not part of the education business and not political or public issues. Actually, they are often labeled as "women's issues."

The assistant principal learns to display a calm dispassionate front and to fit complex dilemma-laden situations into categories that can be sorted out through rules and regulations (recall the research in Chapter 3). While this separation and denial has traditionally affected women more than men, it is problematic for both men and women contemplating the career. It is a loss for school leadership, too, for in the process of learning to focus on rational and publicly defined issues, wiping clean this personal insight and emotional involvement, much is lost.

However, new conceptualizations of leadership acknowledge the value of the personal. Emotionally engaged leadership encompasses the relational ethic of care that emerged from feminist scholarship and the sense that relationships matter in organizational lives (Gilligan, 1982; Noddings, 1992). Caring can be seen as both an activity and a feeling and can be a centerpiece for reframing schooling. Noddings argues that "the first job of the schools is to care for our children. We should educate all our children not only for competence but also for caring. Our aim should be to encourage the growth of competent, caring, loving and lovable people" (Noddings, 1992, p. xiv). Such a philosophical stance fits well with the motivations and philosophies of teachers, who care about children and about each other and who, for many reasons, see teaching as a labor of love (Acker, 1999). Accepting these human connections leads to school leaders feeling grounded in their original educator mission— the one that motivated their career choice, to be near children and help them develop. Whether there is deep spiritual satisfaction, simple joy, or a sense of congruence between one's job and one's sense of being in a caring community, schools led by administrators and teachers who value that human connection will surely make a difference.

Viewing Administration as Leadership of Identity-Negotiation Organizations

What if we acknowledged that for kids, going to school is mainly about finding out who they are, where they belong, where they are going, and how far they can push the boundaries? Recent theorizing about education, especially that which focuses on children who veer from the norm for a variety of reasons, has had to develop this view. Children from immigrant families; English language learners; children with disabilities; those whose sense of their sexuality does not fit with heterosexist norms; and those whose religion, ethnicity, or race is not reflected in the curriculum or the leadership in schools are, of course, searching for evidence of how they can fit in or be somebody in this context. School is a place for sorting this identity-formation. From this perspective, what happens in the shower room after P.E. or in the parking lot may be much more relevant learning for the child than the formal algebra curriculum. As a child is negotiating identity, attendance and compliance with school norms may be a huge struggle!

The literature for teachers, counselors, and psychologists emphasizes identity negotiation. However, administrative texts do little to point leaders to understand children. This is left to the parents, teachers, counselors, and psychologists. This alternative approach would be the most radical challenge to school administration. In essence, leaders would focus on child development, which includes, but is not limited to, academic achievement. Administrators, and especially assistant principals, are definitely coping with child development, identity negation, and family issues every day. However, they do so without training and without formal recognition that this is what is most real to the children, who are supposed to be the focus of schooling.

A related perspective is presented as "Nurturing the development of families' educational cultures" in a University Council for Educational Administration summary of "What We Know about Successful School Leadership" (2003). Recognizing that "student learning is enhanced when it is supported by both the school and the family" (p. 7), the recommendation is for leaders to help strengthen families: promoting trust and communication between families and schools, providing resources to families for parenting, and adjusting school practices to accommodate families' cultures.

A few inroads with strengthening families to strengthen students can be detected in administrative management, but the attempts are small: parent conferences in neighborhoods instead of at schools or buses used in the evening to bring parents to conferences, parenting classes or parent centers after school on one night a week, and computer and/or reading classes in which parents attend with their child to learn the basic skills or the skills needed to extend practice for the child. In spite of these efforts, it is clear these are seen as efficiencies rather than philosophical underpinnings that drive administrative action.

Leadership as Expanding Schools' Social Capital

Administrators often see parents, angry community groups, and student cliques as threats. But group relationships, when their values and passions can be satisfied in schooling tasks, can be tremendous assets. Among students, parents, and educators, there are rich networks of shared values and concerns. These interactions can be seen as assets, as a form of social capital that can be the basis for multiplying capacities and resources. Students have acquired knowledge and information, habits and dispositions that they bring to school. "Their relationships and interactions with parents, community members, and other persons in their social network . . . [can be seen as] social capital" (University Council for Educational Administration, 2003, p. 3). School leaders clever enough to see this as capital rather than as disruption are ahead of the game. With leaders viewing community groups, special interests, and even gangs as social capital, the possibilities for enhancing support and involvement in the tasks of schooling are greatly increased.

Power-Sensitive Leadership

Power is embedded in institutions: legislatures, courts, but also in education professions that categorize humans with labels and make them submissive subjects who must at least appear to accept the labels and rules of those who control and manage them (Foucault, 1977; Ball, 1993). Power is revealed through its backlash and resistance. Active resistance might be the child who yells obscenities at the assistant principal. Passive, silent resistance to power might be the woman who drops out of a male-dominated leadership program. Thus leaders need a particular sensitivity in using power. Sensitized assistant principals recognize the power wielded in their official position, especially power over students but also over teachers and parents. The resistance, backlash, and anger thrown at the assistant principal are, in part, reactions to that exercise of power. Thus assistant principals are just doing their jobs in keeping order, judging teachers' worth, telling students to get back in class, and placing students into categories for special treatment (positive and negative). But in doing so, they are enforcing institutional power arrangements that can provoke resentment.

The deeper problems arise when the power arrangements promote privilege or discriminate unfairly. We assert that schools are bureaucracies that promote fairness and provide equity of access to the "goodies" of society. However, some powerful practices use policies and structures in ways that restrict access, cut off opportunity, and maintain privilege. The disempowered and silenced are kept that way, raising "serious questions about the role of schools in the social and cultural reproduction of social classes, gender roles, and racial and ethnic prejudice" (Anderson, 1989, p. 251).

In their daily work, assistant principals unknowingly engage in a battle between those who would restrict access to knowledge and power to elites and those who seek a more equal and participatory society.

Is This Relevant to You?

What was lost as you learned to rein in your passion on the job?

When and where do you really express your feelings about work?

What were the issues in the times you were advised to keep your personal and professional life separate?

Should it be okay for a professional to show love and joy at work?

Why aren't school days and curriculum centered around identity negotiation—or are they?

Now that you know about social capital, how could you capitalize on it?

Think about times when you chose to not use your power. What affected your choice?

When you see evidence of privileged, powerful, dominant groups at work, should you be angry or try to join them?

Social Justice Leadership

The terms used above, such as critical humanist, transformative, intentional, and feminist, are encompassed in a more inclusive term: social justice. Social justice demands overt and assertive ways of addressing all the inequities that show up in schooling. It demands that leaders attend to barriers due to poverty, class, immigration, religion, ethnicity, race, language, and gender and sexuality, but also to democratic, spiritual, and inclusive dimensions of schooling. Leadership for Social Justice (LSJ) is a group started in the early 2000s among scholars of educational administration who were fed up with equity issues being pushed aside, especially in training and licensure for school administrators (see www.leadershipforsocial justice.org for more information and materials produced by the group). Thus university programs are, increasingly, creating courses, mission statements, and position advertisements using social justice rhetoric. Research, textbooks and other training materials, and professional journals are, more than ever, focusing on ways to overcome barriers and inequities and strive for social justice. For example, *Leadership for Social Justice: Making Revolutions in Education* by Marshall & Oliva (2006) and *Best Leadership Practices for High Poverty Schools* by Lyman & Villani (2004) are two examples of accessible materials for preparation and staff development that enrich administrators' understanding and capacity to think and act toward social justice.

Policy Advocacy Leadership

Current realities create pressures for the assistant principal to calm down and manage disruptions from the community and parents, from students' unmet needs, and from policy pressures (as shown in Chapter 3). Assistant principals learn to avoid deep questioning of the fundamental purposes of schooling. They cannot do anything to encourage groups that mobilize protests about policies and practices or that support outsider groups' demands on their sites. Where there are dilemmas and chronic problems, one must cope. Just don't ask, don't think about it; make a decision or take an action and move on to the next challenge, most assistant principals learn. Thus assistant principals unlearn any shred of activism. As Anderson says, "Social constructions are so tightly legitimated that certain questions are unaskable and certain phenomena remain unobservable," making persistent dilemmas of schools' part in racism, classism, sexism, and poverty perpetuation into nonissues and nonevents (Anderson, 1990, p. 42). The marginal people and the silenced issues—children with disabilities, immigrant families—get pushed aside.

When schools focus primarily on the issues that powerful policymakers value, the needs of the disenfranchised, the silenced, and the more marginal citizens and students do not garner much attention (e.g., child care, prevention of sexual harassment in schools, women's access to school leadership, arts education). On the other hand, in this atmosphere this underclass can garner negative controlling attention (e.g., "welfare mothers," girl gangs, teacher quality), but the issues get defined by those policymakers in ways unconnected to harsh realities, which still leave the individuals and their problems dangling, pushed aside, and inadequately addressed.

When issues don't cause riots (such as girls who remain passive and quiet in classroom discussions, female teachers who don't aspire to be superintendents), they are ignored in policy arenas. They may be viewed as "soft issues" (such as emotion, self-concept, and feelings of inclusion) and pushed aside. Yet think, for example, of how often one observes that family and school relationships affect students' sense that barriers can be overcome, their sense of efficacy in the classroom, and their sense that academic achievement is important. Thus leaders ought to at least explore whether they could do more with families and relationship-building to affect "the achievement gap." Ironically, these issues are deemed important and fundable only if controlled scientific studies demonstrate that there is a tax-sheltered business whose intervention can produce test-score gains.

But policy advocacy leaders demand that the pushed-aside issues be brought front and center for leaders' and policymakers' attention. Recalling "existential moments" (Smith, 2005), Rosa Smith, a retired superintendent, said, "Nothing in my job description as superintendent mentioned incarcerated black youth. I understood clearly that morning that this terrible statistic [84 percent of incarcerated, below 18-year-olds were youth of color] was, in fact, in large part the result of what these youth had experienced in school, and this was all about my job and my leadership . . . and I was reminded of the saying: the education of our children is a matter of life and death" (p. 2). She asserts that if leaders knew that their jobs were about saving lives, then, under their watch, they would make sure that black kids did not begin school lacking social and educational school readiness, would not be taught disproportionately by less-qualified teachers or placed in special education disproportionately, and so on. She proposes strategies such as "public broad-based reciprocal agreements, including mayors and chambers of commerce, for moving together on behalf of students, building a district policy audit, identifying and correcting the policies that lead to inadequate results for the most vulnerable students," and she continues with suggestions of how advocates can gain the assistance of the Harvard Civil Rights Project, The Algebra Project, the Education Trust, and others. Such a social justice advocacy approach, with activist strategies, goes far beyond the all-too-typical managerial approach to leadership.

If we compile the perspectives from the critiques, insights, theories, and models presented above, the new model for leadership can be named Advocacy Leadership. For schools to be led by advocates, their leaders' earliest recruitment and training—on-the-job and in courses and staff development—would need to be quite special. That early experience would begin during their teaching careers, when the most outspoken, critical, and idealistic teachers would be tapped on the shoulder and sponsored both in their districts and in educational administration programs. They would then learn, in experiences ranging from on-the-job activism to master's and doctoral theory and research, the dispositions and skills for purposefully seeking the silenced voices, the unnoticed realities affecting children and families, the insights derived from the perspectives of disenfranchised groups. For such a leader, devoting one's life work to doing advocacy is a radically different school leadership model, as proposed in Marshall & Gerstl-Pepin (2005).

LOOKING AT EQUITY IN THE PROFESSION THROUGH CULTURAL AND POLITICAL LENSES

Something in the culture of school administration locks out most women and minorities. Supported by strong and ancient traditions asserting "women's place" and assumptions that men should not have to subject themselves to female bosses or be paid less than women, those in power keep the power. Supported by cultural preference and strong networks supporting white males, minority educators still face communities ready to undermine their leadership. Educators who are from minority groups can see that only a select few of them will attain leadership positions, and they will often be marginal members of the administrative culture. Conversely, these minority administrators become so ensconced in the culture of the administration that they may also become only marginally associated with their minority culture. Similarly, women in leadership sometimes feel they must act like men to be accepted. A more radical and useful approach to explain and change this lockout comes from adopting a political perspective. Minogue (1983, p. 73) said, "Nothing gets done which is unacceptable to dominant or influential political groups, which may be defined to include the 'bureaucratic leadership' group." Leadership behaviors, activities, values, and attitudes toward women and minorities might be somewhat different—and thus be judged as deficient. To disassemble the lockout requires those in power to give up their exclusive control over the definitions of what is right, proper, and good.

Recent critiques (e.g., Young & Skrla, 2003) have recommended expanded models of leadership, asserting that women's qualities as leaders can, in fact, widen the definitions and demonstrate qualities that can improve schools. Reviews of literature on women in school administration have found consistent patterns in favor of women (Ortiz & Marshall, 1988; Marshall, 1989; Shakeshaft, 1987; Mitchell, 1987; Bell & Chase, 1989): women exert more positive efforts on instructional supervision.

- Women produce more positive interactions with community and staff.
- Women's administrative styles tend to be more democratic, inclusive, and conflict-reducing.
- Female secondary principals engage in more cooperative planning.
- Female elementary principals observe teachers more frequently.
- Female superintendents tour the schools more.
- Female principals and superintendents spend more time in the classroom and in discussions with teachers about instruction and academic content.

Women are less concerned about bureaucracy and are more inclined to spend energy on instructional matters, spend time on counseling and reducing conflict, take more work home, and spend more time in schools and in monitoring instructional programs.

Finally, social psychologists and sociolinguists suggest that women's decision-making is more oriented toward caring for everyone (Gilligan, 1982) and that women's ways of speaking, while less assertive and authoritarian, include more listening and have the effect of eliciting input and participation in groups (see Marshall, 1988, for expansion of this argument).

Such differences would, presumably, favor women's ascendance in an era of school leadership that emphasizes instructional leadership and an openness to teacher involvement in designing the work of schools. For participatory management, teacher empowerment, and instructional leadership, women's leadership should be recruited and supported. As more women have been elected to school boards, more female superintendents have been hired. The power of the female vote in national elections has been well documented, but it may well impact local change as well. With more women making decisions on school boards and in administration, will the values driving the decisions and the leadership styles be different? Parallel arguments regarding minority administrators are emerging from research and policy statements. Studies of the sociology of education in this country during the last 60 years show that careers in education were one of the surest ways for families to move from the underclass to the middle class. That is, education was and is a common route for one generation to shift classes. Think of black families who made their living as sharecroppers who could send one child to college to become a teacher. That next generation develops a middle-class frame of reference and has middle-class experiences as it adopts middle-class values. This experience gives value to the educational process and gives minority administrators whose families have followed these routes a clearer understanding of the profound need for schooling. Such administrators may have managed a jump not only to the middle class but also to the professional class by landing a job as a school administrator.

Understandings of poverty, struggle, and class are powerful tools when working with students who remain in the underclass. Also, "their shared social and cultural experiences as well as their cultural mediation skills they have developed for connection between school and home" (Quiocho & Rios, 2000, p. 488) strengthen their potential as educators in our diverse communities and schools. In practice, African American leaders offer schools the following:

- Principals have a strong commitment to African American students and place higher priority on community involvement (Lomotey, 1989; Pollard, 1997);

- They function as role models encouraging positive student-teacher relationships (Valverde, 1987);
- They look to the community to assist in academic and social change, rather than relying on a Eurocentric focus on the leader's traits (Banks, 1991);
- They are seen by teachers of color to be capable of leading as an ethnic example and accomplishing tasks in the best interests of all, and their relationship bonds are like those of family (although white teachers see them as capable because of their credentials and intellect; Jones, 2002); and
- There is a positive correlation between the number of African Americans in leadership positions and the number of African American teachers employed (Stewart, Meier, & England, 1989).

As Tillman says, "African Americans can help shape the lives of African American students in positive ways that will lead to their social, emotional, academic, professional, and economic excellence" (in press). The same logic (although the research evidence is scarce) applies to thinking about Native American, Hispanic, and other minority leaders, so much needed to expand our views of leadership.

The demand for equity and students' needs for role models are simple and straightforward arguments to end the lockout. But even after decades of "affirmative action," little has changed. Furthermore, numerical representation of underrepresented groups is not the whole story. Newly conceptualized research asks, "How can we enhance our understanding of leadership by studying atypical leaders?" Notice the emphasis on valuing experience rather than searching for the ways these leaders need to change to fit the old models of "typical." African American leaders offer unique educational, racial, and cultural perspectives, and their contributions can enhance theory practice in educational leadership (Tillman, in press). Women's values, perspectives, and attention, as shown above, also offer widened views.

Thus, instead of recommending mere equity (which has not happened), a more radical demand would be to *openly favor* female and minority candidates for school leadership. This would require not only an open recognition by policymakers that women and minorities have had unequal access but also an open assertion that strong representation of women and minorities in leadership is essential for children who need such role models.

Is This Relevant to You?

Suppose you wanted to demonstrate social justice leadership or enact policy advocacy. How could you get other educators to follow your lead?

What is stopping you from joining advocacy groups that have values and interests similar to yours?

What are the most striking examples of when, like Rosa Smith, you saw how very responsible educators are for saving children?

How could you make a case that districts should select female and minority administrators rather than equally qualified white males?

PURPOSEFULLY EXAMINING FUNDAMENTAL DILEMMAS

In an insightful reflection on the role of the assistant principal, Iannaccone (1985) recommended using the assistant as a "window on the building" or a lens for examining the inner workings of the school site. Such microanalysis would, he said, uncover critical and chronic dilemmas in the working of schools because assistants, in their daily work, smooth over those dilemmas and keep things running.

Indeed, the research on assistant principals' assumptive worlds (see Chapter 3) reveals that assistants learn to cope with chronically scarce resources, the need to comply with dominant values and exhibit loyalty within the hierarchical system, the need to distance themselves from teachers and teaching, the need to spend their time covering their bases as defined by the job description even when they see more pressing needs, and so on. In fact, part of their enculturation as administrators is surviving "professional shock" (Marshall, 1985a) as they encounter problems. In one case study, an administrator articulated the array of dilemmas he faced as he tried to decide whether to learn to comply and to reinforce the school system that was so inadequate at meeting students' needs:

You give up after a while, or you just don't want the hassle, the ultimate responsibility. I was anxious for a promotion to principal. But this system, the American system, is not going to support inner-city schools. I know people with money—they don't care about these kids . . . Reagan has no sensitivity to the problems here. We have a good superintendent who *says* we're responsible. But to function in an environment where no one cares but us—why take on the burden? I like the kids and they like me, but I don't see much hope in the total world. Do businesses really want black people to move up in society? I see the potential in kids but in reality, society wants things the way they are. Capitalist society is based on having working people. Society allows us to pick a few to succeed. Yet the superintendent is there cheering us all on; but I have to survive. Power and money don't give a damn. That's why I'm not sure I want to be a principal. The physical plant is falling apart. Do I want the ultimate responsibility for this? Would I want to be a superintendent? The real dream for me is to have money to have some representative outcome for all the input. (Marshall, 1985b, p. 32)

More recently, an assistant principal from Mertz's study said:

Here's what kills you. Everyone agrees when you talk about making change or changing the way you deal with kids. Everyone agrees, even the principal . . . And then, everything stays exactly the same. After awhile you get tired and the things that really go against what you believe, that really violate what you hold dear, then for one kid here or there you do what you think is right and hope you don't get caught. (Mertz, 2005, p. 28)

Entry-level administrators carry on these kinds of inner debates, which bring to the surface the continuous conflicts with teachers and parents, conflicts over curriculum that bores students, and conflicts over student control and discipline systems that denigrate children and include sexism, racism, and classism. Curriculum theorists and critical theorists have laid out the challenge to use schooling to "transform inequitable, undemocratic or oppressive institutions and social relations" (Burbeles & Berk, 1999, p. 57). Teachers encounter, and do their best with, students who are set back by their backgrounds or their lack of fit with school norms. In their leadership positions, assistant principals hope to have the power to make real differences but are often frustrated when dominant societal values don't give a damn.

Currently, school administrators learn to cope with, manage, and often repress discussion about these dilemmas. Assistant principals learn on the job to avoid moral dilemmas, and over time, they learn that "our job is not to question, but to serve" (Mertz, 2005, p. 23). Mentors and sponsors tell them to stop being so sensitive and to pick their battles. Professors teach them about the political structure of schooling so they can better manipulate that structure.

However, these dilemmas could be the source of a powerful critical examination of schooling if they were treated as "windows on the building" for discovery rather than as problems to repress. Retreats aimed at identifying, describing, and creating action plans around such dilemmas could lead to radical change. In a safe environment, far from the demands on their job descriptions and the need to fit into the administrative culture, assistant principals could generate descriptions of what they see going wrong, with facilitators there to lead them to identify strategies for change. Such a process, done in isolation with no thought about the larger system, would be a time-waster at best and could generate distrust and damage careers. But as a national movement aimed at valuing the perspectives of the assistant principal in order to gain a clearer view of the school site, it could work.

REFRAMING AND RE-VISIONING FUNDAMENTAL ASSUMPTIONS OF SCHOOLING

Too often, policies affecting schools are framed with inadequate knowledge of what is really needed at sites. Often they are made and implemented in ways that benefit a few and let others fall through the cracks. Educators gripe about such inadequate policies. To move beyond griping, leaders must do something; they must report and act to enfranchise people and to disrupt and dismantle inadequate, stupid, and oppressive policy directions. The astute leader can provide reports and can act in and around the public arena to provide information for critical reflection on any policy actions, calling attention to "the cultural embeddedness of policies" (Kelly and Maynard-Moody, 1993, p. 138) and creating a forum for multiple truths. The leader then becomes a facilitator of deliberation, bringing together multiple perspectives to explore alternative courses of action and to help people see the limits of their current ways of doing things. The leader's report incorporates the perspectives of key stakeholders and the multiple, conflicting, and negotiated subjective perspectives of people who lay meaning on policies. Such an approach requires extensive data-gathering by a politically astute leader with a moral purpose. This may not eliminate oppressive structures, but the report can help groups raise fundamental questions or get the oppressed to see, label, and articulate their stories, increasing their power in agenda-setting (Freire, 1985; Ryan, 1988). Where policies are working well for all affected, there is no need for reframing. But some ignore the lived realities of educators, children, and families. Some policies' goals are playing havoc with K–12 schooling, especially when they overemphasize individualism, competition, the market, and false meritocracy. The assistant principal, then, can take policies (whether federal NCLB or local classroom reassignments) and set up strategies to reframe and revision policies. Marshall and Gerstl-Pepin (2005) show first the demoralizing and de-skilling policies aimed at ensuring educator quality, which, by the way, focus particularly at women, who are 75 percent of the teaching workforce. They then show the feminist and social justice critique, asserting possibilities of an enlivened, transformative, empowered educator workforce if, for example, the ethic of care, relationship, sense of spiritual/cultural mission, joy, and passion for engaging with children's development could be unleashed, as advocated by feminists and liberation pedagogy, à la Noddings (1984), Hooks (1994), and others. Educators, then, instead of being envisioned in policy designs as controlled cogs in a production function, would be social justice policy advocates, prepared and willing to go to battle when funding and testing policies leave their students behind. School leaders of the future need to be socialized as constant questioners and trained to seek ways to reframe policies and programs that do not work for children and families. When, for example, federal policy targets schools with inequities but the effects are punitive, they need to be able to do more than just complain. NCLB's demands for accounting for and closing gaps in achievement have forced schools to address specific inequities in specific ways. The federal law punishes schools and educators that do not find ways to show achievement gains and reduced dropout rates for minority and poor children.

School leaders, including assistant principals, need to be able to articulate the negative repercussions of such policies. But they also need to be adept at offering alternatives. In doing so, they become real leaders, able to enter the political frays as advocates for children, families, teachers, and themselves.

A true educational leader imbued with social justice values can join teachers and families as they exert political pressure on state legislatures for money, policy, resources, etc. Indeed, what is called for is broader involvement or connection with the people who make up schools (teachers, students, and families) and the passion to advocate in all arenas for changes that advance the schools as community centers and places of hope and support as well as places for teaching and learning.

Once the culture of the profession of school leadership is redefined, assistant principals' connections with the community can be quite different. The social justice leader-in-training, as an assistant principal, would be expected to seek out the marginalized voices, search for and identify unmet needs, and create structures and supports that open school sites for community-inclusive and democratized schooling.

TRAINING FOR NEW METAPHORS AND THEORIES FOR ENACTING LEADERSHIP

The worst training experience for alternative models for leaders is the traditional mix of formal and informal socialization described in Chapter 2. Traditional university programs are closely tied to training and certifying individuals to fit into the professional culture that emphasizes administration as a rational science, with knowledge and expertise centered on bureaucratic management and control. On-the-job training in the knowledge, skills, and values of administration, occurring most intensively in the assistant principalship, aided or not by sponsors and mentors, actually *cripples* the individual's potential to use insights from models of feminist, intentional, critical humanist, and other alternative models. Gandhi, Jane Addams, and Martin Luther King, Jr., would not have survived assistant principalhood; moving into higher leadership would have been out of the question.

Better training experiences would start with the following kinds of components:

1. Critical and feminist theorist professors and scholars in residence and in continuous dialogue with students, local practitioners, and policymakers;

2. History and philosophy of science taught so that when they do research, students understand how their questions are affected by the dominant forces that lend legitimacy to knowledge;

3. Courses in qualitative inquiry so that students acquire skills in uncovering the individual and subjective nature of the meanings that people make as they view events;

4. Courses on the history of organizations and institutions, especially schools, so that students understand the social forces that structured our current systems of schooling;

5. Courses on the social context of schooling so that students see the economic, sociocultural, and political webs within which schooling takes place;

6. Internships in very different organizations (e.g., child-centered British schools; the Ministry of Education in, for example, Israel, South Africa, or China; social welfare agencies) so that students see different models of organizations and leadership, different goals, and the workings of organizations that connect with and affect the lives of children;

7. Internships in schools that have successfully created new structures (e.g., teacher and parent decision-making, schools within schools, flattened management, peer-teacher supervision and evaluation) and schools with different philosophies (e.g., Montessori or other child-centered schools, charter schools, private schools, or magnet schools with special cultures and specialized purposes);

8. Support for exploring in an interdisciplinary mode (e.g., a minor in anthropology, social work, political science, law, early childhood, public health);

9. Courses preparing educational leaders to work toward equity goals (for suggestions, see Marshall & Oliva, 2006; Marshall, 1989; Shapiro & Parker, 1989);

10. Courses aimed at assisting leaders in identifying and articulating their values and developing appropriate action plans and career strategies;

11. Courses applying different metaphors of management; drawing implications for leaders' activities, attitudes, and behaviors; and discussing ways that the different metaphors would affect the structures of the daily lives of school participants (e.g., using Gareth Morgan's text, 1986);

12. Requirements that prospective and current school leaders immerse themselves in situations where they are total outsiders. Journeys into uncomfortable, foreign, even hostile territory, where they must devise their own strategies to adjust, where they must negotiate, compromise, or even hide aspects of their identity in order to be allowed to be there, will provide leaders with personal and emotional insights into the struggles of those who are minorities and marginalized because of their family or cultural backgrounds (see Laible, 2000); and

13. Budgets for schooling set up, as they are in business and the military, with the assumption that educators' advanced professional education will be paid for, not come out of the personal pockets of the ones who could find ways to afford it.

Such approaches would be declared impractical. They would fly in the face of current proposals from the University Council for Educational Administration, most state legislatures, and administrators' professional organizations. They would make most superintendents uncomfortable.

However, such approaches would educate potential school leaders in critically examining tradition and identifying new organizational arrangements to enhance the efficacy of schooling for all. They would also demand that communities recognize and support a new model of leadership. Instead of the quick-decision, in-charge paternalist who works with the local power structure, this leader would not command. Instead of calling teachers and parents in for a day of being empowered in decision-making, she would create structures to include others in framing issues for debate. It would take longer and be a more ambiguous process, but it should lead to an enhanced sense of ownership in the goals and processes. It would lead educators and their constituents to make demands that would embarrass powerful people, but it has the potential to get beyond quick and cheap reforms and ask deeper questions (such as, "What values support a political system that provides tax breaks for the wealthy but cuts school lunch programs?").

Instead of accepting the traditional bureaucratic model, the new and different leader might work within a metaphor or model of the organization as a family, a network, or a kinship system. Instead of assuming that schooling should help kids learn to compete and win, this new leader might raise questions about whether the curriculum should emphasize team building and cooperative work. The assistant principal position is a great place for supporting such new leadership.

Is This Relevant to You?

What will you do to find ways to retrain yourself—and bring others along with you?

How will you get past the fear of being different, of getting fired?

How will you face fundamental dilemmas without becoming depressed?

What are possible ways to seek or create groups of people interested in rethinking purposes of schooling?

What societal changes would support school leaders who enacted these alternative styles of leadership?

SUMMARY

This chapter proposes a variety of plans for improving the assistant principalship. It offers several ideas for rethinking the structure of hierarchy and roles in the system. It identifies ways to alter structures in educational systems to affect assistant principals' training and selection, their satisfaction and support, and their ability to cope. Our suggestions would expand the functions, provide support and rewards, and advance equity in the assistant principalship. Some school districts may have experimented with similar plans and made attempts to alter and improve the position. They should share their ideas in articles in educators' journals and at conferences. It is important, however, that all alterations be analyzed to assess not only the immediate benefits but also the positive and negative spin-off effects. Another caution: Ideas developed in one setting may have different effects in another setting.

This chapter, then, offers stimulating and sometimes challenging new ways to think about leadership. They may seem scary and overly daunting, perhaps not practical for those who just want to survive within the status quo. They may seem impossible for people at such "low" levels of administration. But such different ways of conceptualizing leadership for the assistant principal can be the very best experience in the early socialization of a new kind of leader. Furthermore, these different approaches could entice more diverse and energetic new recruits into school leadership, just when they are so very needed. Our focus on the assistant principal role offers possibilities for critical interventions that can result in far-reaching improvements in all aspects of schooling. Preparing assistant principals well is ensuring a different future for schools, students, and families. In many cases, it is about life and death.

One final thought: Assistant principals still find delights within the dilemmas of their days. Below, middle school assistant principal Mr. Mutillo smiles as he recalls a sixth grader's understanding of NCLB:

As a little sixth grader came strolling down the breezeway this morning on her way from the school bus, I overheard her conversation with a few other students. I heard her thinking aloud: "Children left behind, child behind, no child left?" Finally she pronounced "No child left behind" as she arrived within talking distance next to me. She asked, "Isn't that a law or something?" I said, "Sort of." The sixth grader stated, "Cool, that means I ain't getting held back in sixth grade this year." After I stopped smiling, I told her, "That's not quite what it means; you still have to pass your grade." She seemed disheartened. But she made me smile, despite the poignancy.

DISCUSSION QUESTIONS AND ACTIVITIES

1. List examples of quick-fix and Band-Aid approaches to altering schools and school leadership that you have encountered, and then discuss how they do and do not work.

2. Form a group of four or more assistant principals from within and beyond your school. First, lead a discussion based on the issues raised in this book. Then, ask the group whether they want to continue to get together, and consider actions ranging from a monthly "whine and wine" group to making presentations to the school board, to wider ranging strategies as in number 3 below.

3. Meet with representatives from your statewide professional association and generate a public relations, media, and research plan for highlighting the importance and value of assistant principals. Consider expanding this to be a nationwide effort, perhaps with foundation funding.

4. Divide your group into sections, each of which is assigned the task of articulating and defending one of the alternative models of leadership (e.g., one group articulates and defends social justice leadership, one does intentional leadership, and so on). As each group does this, others play the devil's advocate, arguing against the model. It should get lively!

5. Often theories and research are written in ways that are off-putting and ponderous. Through libraries and the Internet, find and read two of the original sources cited in the above section on alternative models and write a five-page version of the author's ideas. Write it in a format that can be submitted to a practitioner journal such as *NASSP Bulletin*. Publishing such works could be a real service to educators looking for new ideas.

6. As in number 5 above, use the original source to write a five-page paper that frames a situation in your district or school according to the critical theory.

7. Prepare an outline of the alternative models for leadership. Then meet with the person in your district who makes decisions about administrator staff development and discuss the

possibility of collaborating with him or her in a workshop. Consider putting together teams of teachers, assistant principals, principals, and central office administrators in the workshop.

8. Go back to activity number 3 in Chapter 2. After reading Chapter 5, how would you now write job descriptions that entice good teachers into the assistant principal position?

9. Investigate with your state department of education and administrators' association whether they have data on the gender and race of assistant principals. If not, begin a campaign to get your state, then others, to collect and publish such data.

10. Keep a journal in which you write reflections on the times when you, or someone you observed, seemed to be enacting some form of alternative leadership. Send them to the author at marshall@email.unc.edu for possible inclusion in the next edition of this book. Your confidentiality will be protected.

11. Identify actions you have taken as an assistant principal that were framed or informed by one of the alternative leadership models discussed in this chapter. Explain what you were thinking when you acted as you did.

12. This chapter asserts that quick fixes and Band-Aid approaches will not be effective until we look at equity through cultural and political lenses. Lead a group discussion of your experiences with the "quick-fix" approaches related to increasing access for women and minorities to administrative careers. Then discuss what would need to happen in your district, your professional association, and your university preparation to move beyond quick fixes and get at a cultural and political approach to equity in school administration.

13. Throughout this book, we assert that the assistant principal faces constant shocks revealing fundamental dilemmas in schooling. After a group discussion, consider keeping a journal of these shocks. Not only could it be cathartic but it could also be useful in the next edition of this book. Feel free to e-mail marshall@email.unc.edu if you feel comfortable

with sharing such insights (we reiterate: confidentiality will be protected).

14. Identify what special skills and perspectives you would expect to see if there were more access to administration for women and minorities. Identify a specific underrepresented group (African American women, gays or lesbians, individuals with disabilities, etc.) and describe a point of view and skill set that would enrich an administrative team by including that person.

15. Although there are many suggestions in this chapter, the authors are hopeful that some reform and restructuring is taking place in schools and districts. Identify something that your district or school is doing that supports some of the directions identified in Chapter 5. How have you been involved in those efforts or how could you get involved?

References

Abney, E. (1978). The effects of desegregation on the professional job status of public school principals employed in Florida. *Cross Reference, 3*(1), 239–258.

Acker, S. (1990). Managing the drama: The head teacher's work in an urban primary school. *The Sociological Review, 38(2),* 247–271.

Acker, S. (1999a). Carry on caring: The work of women teachers. *British Journal of Sociology of Education, 16(1),* 21–36.

Acker, S. (1999b). *The realities of teachers' work: Never a dull moment* London: Continuum.

Allison, P. A., & Allison, D. J. (1989). Playing PACman: Principal assessment centers as an addictive innovation. *American Sociological Review, 25,* 855–867. (ERIC Document Reproduction Service No. ED306666, CHN EA 020 912).

Anderson, G. L. (1989). Critical ethnography in education: Origins, current status, and new direction. *Review of Educational Research, 59(3),* 249–270.

Anderson, G. L. (1990). Toward a critical constructivist approach to school administration: Invisibility, legitimation, and the study of non-events. *Educational Administration Quarterly, 26,* 38–59.

Armstrong, L. (2004). The secondary assistant principal in the state of Texas: Duties and job satisfaction (University of Houston). *Dissertation Abstracts International, 65(02),* 353. [Electronic version]. Retrieved March 25, 2005, from http://wwwlib.umi.com/dissertations/ fullcit/3122339

Association of California School Administrators. (2001, June). *Recruitment and retention of school leaders: A critical need.* ACSA Task Force on Administrator Shortage.

Austin, D. B., & Brown, H. L., Jr. (1970). *Report of the assistant principalship of the study of the secondary school principalship.* Reston, VA: National Association of Secondary School Principals.

Ball, T. (1993). New faces of power. In T. Wartenberg (Ed.), *Rethinking power.* Albany: State of New York University Press.

Banks, C. (1991). *City school superintendents: Their career patterns, traits, and perceptions of leadership and managerial skills and style.* Unpublished doctoral dissertation, Seattle University.

Bartholomew, S. K., & Fusarelli, L. D. (2003). Reconnecting preparation and practice through the work lives of assistant principals. In F. C. Lunenburg & C. S. Carr (Eds.), *Shaping the future* (pp. 291–300). Lanham, MD: Scarecrow Education.

Beatty, B. (2000). The emotions of educational leadership: Breaking the silence. *International Journal of Leadership in Education, 3(4),* 331–357.

Belenky, M. F., Clinchy, B. M., Goldberger, N. R., & Tarule, J. M. (1986). *Women's ways of knowing: The development of self, voice, and mind.* New York: Basic Books.

Bell, C. S., & Chase, S. E. (1989, March). *Women as leaders in a male-dominated context.* Paper presented at the annual meeting of the American Educational Research Association, San Francisco.

Berger, P., & Luckmann, T. (1967). *The social construction of reality.* Garden City, NY: Anchor.

Berman, P., & McLaughlin, M. (1978). *Federal programs supporting educational changes: Vol. 8. Implementing and sustaining innovation.* Santa Monica, CA: Rand Corporation.

Black, A. B. (1978). *Secondary assistant principals: Their roles as perceived by self, supervisors, peers, and subordinates.* Unpublished doctoral dissertation, Temple University.

Black, B. (2002, February). An insider's view: An assistant principal's diary illustrates why the job is so difficult. *American School Board Journal,* 37–38.

Blount, J. M. (2003, April). *Mandatory marriage for male superintendents, 1880–2000 (Gay/lesbian/bisexual/transgender school leaders: Historical, legal, and empirical perspectives).* Paper presented at the meeting of the American Educational Research Association, Chicago.

Bolman, L. G., & Deal, T. E. (1984). *Modern approaches to understanding and managing organizations.* San Francisco: Jossey-Bass.

Bosk, C. (1979). *Forgive and remember: Managing medical failure.* Chicago: University of Chicago Press.

Bossert, S. T., Dwyer, D. C., Rowan, B., & Lee, G. V. (1982). The instructional management role of the principal. *Educational Administration Quarterly, 18(3),* 34–64.

Boyd, W. J. (1983). *Political science and educational administration: Rethinking educational policy and management in the 1980s.* Deakin, Australia: Deakin University Press.

Bredeson, P. V. (1988). Perspectives on schools: Metaphors and management in education. *Journal of Educational Administration, 26(3),* 293–310.

Bridges, E., & Baehr, M. (1971). The future of administrator selection procedure. *Administrator's Notebook, 19,* 1–4.

Browne-Ferrigno, T. (2003). Becoming a principal: Role conception, initial socialization, role identity, transformation, purposeful engagement. *Educational Administration Quarterly, 39(4),* 468–503.

Browning Public Schools. (1999). *Job description—Assistant principal.* Browning, MT: Author.

Burbeles, N. C., & Berk, R. (1999). Critical thinking and critical pedagogy: Relations, differences, and limits. In T. S. Popkewitz & L. Fendler (Eds.), *Critical theories in education: Changing terrains of knowledge and politics* (pp. 45–65). New York: Routledge.

Burns, J. (1978). *Leadership.* New York: Harper & Row.

Calabrese, R. L., & Adams, C. F. (1987). A comparative analysis of alienation among secondary school administrators. *Planning and Changing, 18(2),* 90–97.

Carlson, R. O. (1972). *School superintendents: Careers and performance.* Columbus, OH: Charles E. Merrill.

Clark, D. L., & Meloy, J. M. (1988). Renouncing bureaucracy: A democratic structure for leadership in schools. In T. J. Sergiovanni & J. Moore (Eds.), *Schooling for tomorrow: Directing reforms to issues that count* (pp. 272–294). Boston: Allyn & Bacon.

Collegegrad.com. (2005, February 18). *Career information: Education administrators.* Retrieved March 25, 2005, from http://www.collegegrad.com/careers/manag08.shtml

Coursen, D. (1975, June). Women and minorities in administration. *School Leadership Digest,* 1–26.

Coursen, D. (1989). Two special cases: Women and blacks. In S. Smith & P. Piele (Eds.), *School leadership: Handbook for excellence* (2nd ed., pp. 85–106). Eugene, OR.

Cranston, N., Tromans, C., & Reugebrink, M. (2004). Forgotten leaders: What do we know about the deputy principalship in secondary schools. *International Journal of Leadership in Education, 7,* 225–242.

Croft, J. C., & Morton, J. L. (1977, April). *The assistant principal: In quandary or comfort?* Paper presented at the annual meeting of the American Educational Research Association, New York.

Crow, G. M., Mecklowitz, B., & Weekes, Y. N. (1992). *From teaching to administration: A preparation institute.* Lancaster, PA: Technomic.

Crowson, R., & Porter-Gehrie, C. (1980). Discretionary behavior of principals in large city schools. *Education Administration Quarterly, 16(1),* 46–69.

Cuban, Larry. (1988). *The managerial imperative and the practice of leadership in schools.* Albany: State University of New York Press.

Dobbs, Michael. (2004, February 22). Spared the rod, lost his job. *The News & Observer,* p. 7A.

Downing, C. R. (1983, April). *Enhancing the elementary school assistant principalship: Some findings from research.* Paper presented at the annual meeting of the American Educational Research Association, Knoxville, TN.

Educational Research Service. (1998). *Is there a shortage of qualified candidates for openings in the principalship?* Arlington, VA: Author.

Educational Research Service. (2004). *Salaries and wages paid professional and support personnel in public schools, 2003–2004.* Arlington, VA: Author.

Edwards, A. T. (1993). *The female high school principal in Fairfield County, Connecticut.* Unpublished doctoral dissertation, Teachers College, Columbia University.

Elshtain, J. B. (1997). *Real politics: At the center of everyday life.* Baltimore: The Johns Hopkins University Press.

Equal Employment Opportunity Commission. (1974). [Elementary-secondary staff information (EEO-5) annual survey]. Unpublished data. Washington, DC: Government Printing Office.

Equal Employment Opportunity Commission. (1976). [Elementary-secondary staff information (EEO-5) annual survey]. Unpublished data. Washington, DC: Government Printing Office.

Equal Employment Opportunity Commission. (1978). [Elementary-secondary staff information (EEO-5) annual survey]. Unpublished data. Washington, DC: Government Printing Office.

Faludi, S. (1991). *Backlash: The undeclared war against American women.* New York: Crown.

Fenwick, L. T., & Pierce, M. C. (2001). *Professional development of principals.* Washington, DC: ERIC Clearinghouse on Teaching and Teacher Education.

Ferguson, K. E. (1984). *The feminist case against bureaucracy.* Philadelphia: Temple University.

Fiore, Thomas A. (1997). *Public and private school principals in the United States [microform]: A statistical profile, 1987–88 to 1993–94.* Washington, DC: National Center for Education Statistics, U.S. Department of Education, Office of Educational Research and Improvement, Educational Resources Information Center.

Floyd, M. K. (1987, April). *Flexibility and central office supervisors: The instrumental function of fragmentation, invisibility, and ambiguity.* Paper presented at the annual meeting of the American Educational Research Association, Washington, DC.

Follett, M. P. (1978). The giving of orders. In J. Shafritz & A. Hyde (Eds.), *Classics of public administration* (pp. 29–37). Oak Park, IL: Moore. (Original work published 1926).

Foster, W. (1986). *Paradigms and promises: New approaches to educational administration.* Buffalo, NY: Prometheus.

Foucault, M. (1977). *Discipline and punishment: The birth of the prison.* London: Allen Lane, Penguin.

Freire, P. (1985). *The politics of education: Culture, power, and liberation.* South Hadley, MA: Bergin and Harvey.

Fulton, O. K. (1987). Basic competencies of the assistant principal. *NASSP Bulletin, 71(501),* 52–54.

Gaertner, K. N. (1980). The structure of organizational careers. *Sociology of Education, 53,* 7–20.

Gallant, T. F. (1980). The vice principalship: An important step on the administrative career ladder. *NASSP Bulletin, 64(440),* 28–32.

Gates, S. M., Ringel, J. S., Santibañez, L., & Brown, A. (2004, Summer). Careers of school leaders: What state and district policy makers need to know. *ERS Spectrum,* 39–49.

Georgia State Department of Education. (1983). *Handbook for the Georgia Teacher Certification Test.* Atlanta, GA: Author.

Gilligan, C. (1982). *In a different voice: Psychological theory and women's development.* Cambridge, MA: Harvard University Press.

Giroux, H. (1988). *Schooling and the struggle for public life: Critical pedagogy in the modern age.* Minneapolis: University of Minnesota Press.

Glanz, J. (1994). Redefining the roles and responsibilities of assistant principals. *The Clearing House, 67(5),* 283–287.

Gomez, J. J. (1985). *The evaluation of the management assessment center* (Final report). Miami, FL: Dade County Public Schools.

Gorton, R. A. (1987). Improving the assistant principalship: The principal's contribution. *NASSP Bulletin, 71(501),* 1–4.

Gorton, R. A., & McIntyre, K. E. (1978). *The senior high school principalship: Vol. 2. The effective principal.* Reston, VA: National Association of Secondary School Principals.

Gorton, R. A., Schneider, G. T., & Fisher, J. C. (1988). *The encyclopedia of school administration and supervision.* Phoenix, AZ: ORYX.

Grady, M. L. (2004). *20 biggest mistakes principals make and how to avoid them.* Thousand Oaks, CA: Corwin.

Graham, H. (1991). The concept of caring in feminist research: The case of domestic service. *Sociology, 25(1),* 61–78.

Greenfield, T. B. (1986, April). *Representing organization theory with a human face: The search for a human and humane understanding of administration.* Paper presented at the annual meeting of the American Educational Research Association, San Francisco.

Greenfield, W. D. (1984, April). *Research on the assistant principal.* Paper presented at the annual meeting of the American Educational Research Association, New Orleans, LA.

Greenfield, W. D. (1985a). Studies of the assistant principalship: Toward new avenues of inquiry. *Education and Urban Society, 18(1),* 7–23.

Greenfield, W. D. (1985b). Developing an instructional role for the assistant principal. *Education and Urban Society, 18(1),* 85–92.

Gross, R. A. (1987). *The vice principal and the instructional leadership role in the public senior high school.* Unpublished doctoral dissertation, University of Pennsylvania.

Hargreaves, A. (1997). *Rethinking educational change with heart and mind.* Alexandria, VA: Association for Curriculum and Development.

Harris, S., Alford, B., & Ballenger, J. (Eds.). (2005). *Women as school executives—Leadership: A bridge to ourselves.* Austin, TX: Texas Council of Women School Executives.

Hartzell, G. N., Williams, R. C., & Nelson, K. T. (1995). *New voices in the field: The work lives of first-year assistant principals.* Thousand Oaks, CA: Corwin.

Harvey, M. J. (1994). The deputy principalship: Retrospect and prospect. *International Journal of Educational Management, 8,* 15–25.

Hausman, C., Nebeker, A., McCreary, J., & Donaldson, D. (2001). The worklife of the assistant principal. *Journal of Educational Administration, 40(2),* 136–157.

Haven, E., Adkinson, P., & Bagley, M. (1980). *Minorities in educational administration: The principalship.* Washington, DC: National Institute of Education.

Hess, F. (1985). The socialization of the assistant principal from the perspective of the local school district. *Education and Urban Society, 18(1),* 93–106.

Hooks, B. (1994). *Teaching to transgress—Education as the practice of freedom.* New York: Routledge.

Hooley, R. M. (1997). *Site-based management, styles of goal accomplishment, and diversity: Hiring and promotional practices among North Carolina assistant principals.* Unpublished doctoral dissertation, Teachers College, Columbia University.

Hughes, M. S. (1988). Developing leadership potential for minority women. In M. Sagaria (Ed.), *Empowering women: Leadership development on campus* (pp. 63–74). San Francisco: Jossey-Bass.

Iannaccone, L. (1985). Vice-principal research: A window on the building. *Education and Urban Society, 18(1),* 121–130.

Johnson, R. S. (2002). *Using data to close the achievement gap—How to measure equity in our schools.* 2nd ed. of *Setting our sights: Measuring equity in school change.* Thousand Oaks, CA: Corwin.

Jones, C. (2002). Teachers' perceptions of African American principals' leadership in urban schools. *Peabody Journal of Education, 77(1),* 7–34.

Jones, E., & Montenegro, X. (1990). *Women and minorities in school administration: Facts and figures, 1989–1990.* Arlington, VA: American Association of School Administrators.

Kahn, R. L., Wolfe, D. M., Quinn, R. P., & Snock, J. D. (1964). *Organizational stress: Studies in role conflict and ambiguity.* New York: John Wiley.

Kaye, E. (2002). *Requirements for certification of librarians, administrators for elementary and secondary schools.* Chicago: University of Chicago Press.

Kelly, G. (1987). The assistant principalship as a training ground for the principalship. *NASSP Bulletin, 71(501),* 13–20.

Kelly, M., & Maynard-Moody, S. (1993). Policy analysis in the post-positivist era: Engaging stakeholders in evaluating the economic development districts program. *Public Administration Review, 53,* 135–142.

Killeen Independent School District. (2001). *Job description—Assistant principal.* Killeen, TX: Author.

Killion, J. (2002, Winter). Aim high and reach out for support. *Journal of Staff Development,* 64–65.

Laible, J. (2000). Loving epistemology: What I hold critical in my life, faith, and profession. *International Journal of Qualitative Studies in Education, 13,* 683–692.

Lawson, T. J. (1970). *A study of the characteristics and functions of assistant principals in Missouri public secondary schools.* Unpublished doctoral dissertation, University of Missouri–Columbia.

Lee, V., Smith, J., & Cioci, M. (1993). Teachers and principals: Gender-related perceptions of leadership and power in secondary schools. *Educational Evaluation and Policy Analysis, 15(2),* 153–180.

Little, J. W. (1984). Seductive images and organizational realities in professional development. *Teachers College Record, 86(1),* 84–102.

Lomotey, K. (1989). *African-American principals: School leadership and success.* New York: Greenwood.

Lortie, D. C. (1975). *Schoolteacher: A sociological study.* Chicago: University of Chicago Press.

Lovelady-Dawson, F. (1980). Women and minorities in the principalship: Career opportunities and problems. *NASSP Bulletin, 64,* 18–28.

Lovely, S. D. (2001, November). Leadership scaffolds for an administrative career ladder. *The School Administrator,* 42–43.

Lyman, L., & Villani, C. (2004). *Best leadership practices for high poverty schools.* Lanham, MA: Rowan & Littlefield Education.

March, J. G., & Simon, H. A. (1958). *Organizations.* New York: Macmillan.

Marshall, C. (1979). *Career socialization of women in school administration.* Unpublished doctoral dissertation, University of California, Santa Barbara.

Marshall, C. (1984). *Surveying the assistant principal's needs.* Unpublished manuscript, University of Pennsylvania.

Marshall, C. (1985a). Professional shock: The enculturation of the assistant principal. *Education and Urban Society, 18(1),* 28–58.

Marshall, C. (1985b). Facing fundamental dilemmas in education systems. *Education and Urban Society, 18(1),* 131–134.

Marshall, C. (1988). Analyzing the culture of school leadership. *Education and Urban Society, 20(3),* 262–275.

Marshall, C. (1989). More than black face and skirts: New leadership to confront the major dilemmas in education. *Agenda, 1(4),* 4–11.

Marshall, C. (1992). School administrators' values: A focus on atypicals. *Educational Administration Quarterly, 28(3),* 368–386.

Marshall, C. (1993). *The unsung role of the career assistant principal.* Reston, VA: National Association of Secondary School Principals.

Marshall, C. (Ed.). (1990). *The role of the assistant principal.* Bloomington, IN: Phi Delta Kappa.

Marshall, C. (Ed.). (1997). *Feminist critical policy analysis—A perspective from primary and secondary schooling.* London: The Falmer Press.

Marshall, C., & Gerstl-Pepin, C. (2005). *Re-framing educational politics for social justice.* Boston: Allyn & Bacon.

Marshall, C., & Mitchell, B. (1989, March). *Women's careers as a critique of the administrative culture.* Paper presented at the annual meeting of the American Educational Research Association, San Francisco.

Marshall, C., & Mitchell, B. (1991). The assumptive worlds of fledgling administrators. *Education and Urban Society, 23(4),* 396–415.

Marshall, C., Mitchell, B., & Gross, R. (1994). A typology of the assistant principalship: A model of orientation to the administrative career. *Advances in educational administration: Vol. 3. New directions in educational administration: Policy, preparation, and practice.* Greenwich, CT: JAI Press.

Marshall, C., & Oliva, M. (2006). *Leadership for social justice: Making revolutions in education.* Boston: Allyn & Bacon.

Marshall, C., Patterson, J. A., Rogers, D. L., & Steele, J. R. (1996, April). Caring as career: An alternative perspective for educational administration. *Educational Administration Quarterly, 32,* 271–294.

Marshall, C., & Ward, M. (2004). Strategic policy for social justice training for leadership. *Journal of School Leadership, 14,* 530–563.

McCarthy, M., & Zent, A. (1982). School administrators: A profile. *Educational Digest, 47,* 28–31.

McIntyre, K. (1966). *Selection of educational administrators.* Columbus, OH: University Council for Educational Administration.

MEEMIC Insurance Co. (2005). MASSP Assistant Principal of the Year. MEEMIC Insurance Company Web site. Retrieved March 25, 2005, from http://www.meemic.com/commasyrCKR.htm

Merton, R. K. (1960). The search for professional status: Sources, costs, and consequences. *American Journal of Nursing, 70,* 662–664.

Mertz, N. (2005). *How it works: Organizational socialization of assistant principals.* Manuscript submitted for publication.

Mertz, N. T., & McNeely, S. R. (1999). *Through the looking glass: An upfront and personal look at the world of the assistant principal.* Paper presented at the annual meeting of the American Educational Research Association, Montreal, Quebec, Canada.

Meyer, J. W., & Rowan, B. (1978). The structure of educational organizations. In M. W. Meyer, et al. (Eds.), *Environments and organizations* (pp. 78–109). San Francisco: Jossey-Bass.

Milstein, M., & Fiedler, C. K. (1988, April). *The status and potential for administrative assessment centers in education.* Paper presented at the annual meeting of the American Educational Research Association, New Orleans, LA.

Minogue, M. (1983). Theory and practice in public policy and administration. *Policy and Politics, 11(1),* 63–85.

Mitchell, B. A. (1987). *Modes for managing the assistant principalship: Sex differences in socialization, role orientation and mobility of public secondary school assistant principals.* Unpublished doctoral dissertation, University of Pennsylvania, Philadelphia.

Mitchell, D. (1983). *Metaphors of management or how far from outcomes can you get?* Unpublished paper, University of California, Riverside.

Morgan, G. (1986). *Images of organization.* Beverly Hills, CA: Sage.

Mueller, F., & Lee, G. V. (1989). Changes abound when peers become PALS. *School Administrator, 46(2),* 16–18.

National Association of Secondary School Principals (NASSP). (1987). *Recognizing the dynamic role of assistant principals.* Reston, VA: Author.

National Association of Secondary School Principals (NASSP). (1991). *Restructuring the assistant principal.* Reston, VA: Author.

National Association of Secondary School Principals (NASSP). (2005). *Developing the 21st century school principal.* Reston, VA: Author.

Noddings, N. (1984). *Caring.* New York: Teachers College Press.

Noddings, N. (1992). *The challenge to care in schools: An alternative approach to education.* New York: Teachers College Press.

Norton, M. S., & Kriekard, J. A. (1987). Real and ideal competencies for the assistant principal. *NASSP Bulletin, 71(501),* 23–30.

Ortiz, F. I. (1982). *Career patterns in education: Women, men and minorities in school administration.* New York: Praeger.

Ortiz, F. I., & Marshall, C. (1988). Women in educational administration. In N. Boyan (Ed.), *Handbook of research on educational administration* (pp. 123–142). New York: Longman.

Pellicer, L. O., Anderson, L. W., Keefe, J. W., Kelly, E. A., & McLeary, L. E. (1988). *High school leaders and their schools: Vol. I. A national profile.* Reston, VA: National Association of Secondary School Principals.

Peterson, K. D., Marshall, C., & Grier, T. (1987). Academies for assistant principals. *Educational Leadership, 45(1),* 47–48.

Pitts, D. (1974). *The role of the public secondary school assistant principal in Virginia.* Unpublished doctoral dissertation, University of Virginia.

Pollard, D. (1997). Race, gender, and educational leadership: Perspectives from African-American principals. *Educational Policy, 11,* 353–374.

Poppink, S., & Shen, J. (2003). Secondary principals' salaries: A national, longitudinal study. *NASSP Bulletin, 87(634),* 67–82.

Porter, J. J. (1996). What is the role of the middle school assistant principal and how should it change? *NASSP Bulletin, 80(578),* 25–29.

Prestine, N. A., & Thurston, P. W. (Eds.). (1994). *Advances in educational administration: Vol. 3. New directions in educational administration: Policy, preparation, and practice.* Greenwich, CT: JAI Press.

Preston, J. F. (1973). *The assistant principalship in the large high school.* Unpublished doctoral dissertation, University of Illinois at Urbana-Champaign.

Prolman, S. (1982). Gender, career paths, and administrative perceptions. *Administrator's Notebook, 30(5),* 1–4.

Prunty, J. J. (1984). *A critical reformulation of educational policy analysis.* Victoria, Australia: Deakin University.

Purpel, D. E. (1999). *Moral outrage in education.* New York: Peter Lang.

Quiocho, A., & Rios, F. (2000). The power of their presence: Minority group teachers and schooling. *Review of Educational Research, 70(4),* 485–528.

Reed, D. B. (1984). *The work of the secondary vice principalship: A field study.* Paper presented at the annual meeting of the American Educational Research Association, New Orleans, LA.

Reed, D. B., & Connors, D. A. (1982). The vice principalship in urban high schools: A field study. *Urban Education, 16(4),* 465–481.

Reed, D. B., & Himmler, A. H. (1985). The work of the secondary assistant principalship: A field study. *Education and Urban Society, 18(1),* 59–84.

Rich, A. (1979). *On lies, secrets and silence.* New York: Norton.

Sarasota County School District. (2001). *Job description—Assistant principal.* Sarasota, FL: Author.

Schainker, S. (2004). *Master's comprehensive exam.* Unpublished document, School of Education, University of North Carolina, Chapel Hill.

Schein, E. H. (1978). *Career dynamics: Matching individual and organizational needs.* Reading, MA: Addison-Wesley.

Schein, E. H. (1985). *Organizational culture and leadership.* San Francisco: Jossey-Bass.

Scheurich, J. J., & Skrla, L. (2003). *Leadership for equity and excellence: Creating high-achievement classrooms, schools, and districts.* Thousand Oaks, CA: Corwin.

Schmitt, N., Noe, R., Meritt, R., Fitzgerald, M., & Jorgensen, C. (1984). *Criterion-related and content-related validity of the NASSP Assessment Center.* Reston, VA: National Association of Secondary School Principals.

Schnittjer, C. J., & Flippo, R. F. (1984). *Competency based certification of school administrators: The Georgia experience.* Paper presented at the annual conference of the American Educational Research Association, New Orleans, LA.

Scott, D. (1989). *Examining the role of the assistant principal: Role orientation, task assignment, and upward mobility of the public secondary assistant principal.* Unpublished doctoral dissertation, University of Pennsylvania, Philadelphia.

Shakeshaft, C. (1987). *Women in educational administration.* Thousand Oaks, CA: Corwin Press.

Shapiro, J. P., & Parker, L. (1989). Preparation of educational administrators for the 21st century: Graduate student voices on the issues of diversity. In *The importance of being pluralistic: Improving the preparation of school administrators (Notes on Reform No. 6).* Charlottesville, VA: National Policy Board for Educational Administration.

Shen, J., Cooley, V. E., & Ruhl-Smith, C. D. (1999). Entering and leaving school administrative positions. *International Journal of Leadership in Education, 2,* 353–367.

Shockley, R. E., & Smith, D. D. (1981). The co-principal: Looking at realities. *The Clearing House, 55,* 90–93.

Sigford, J. L. (2005). *Who said school administration would be fun? Coping with a new emotional and social reality* (2nd ed.). Thousand Oaks, CA: Corwin Press.

Smith, R. A. (2005). Saving Black boys: Unimaginable outcomes for the most vulnerable students require imaginable leadership. *The School Administrator, 1.*

Retrieved from www.aasa.org/publications/saarticledetail.cfm?ItemNumber=949 &snItemNumber=950&tnItemNumber=951

Spady, W. G. (1985). The vice principal as an agent of instructional reform. *Education and Urban Society, 18(1),* 107–120.

Stewart, J., Jr., Meier, K. J., & England, R. E. (1989). In quest of role models: Change in Black teacher representation in urban school districts, 1968–1986. *Journal of Negro Education, 58,* 140–152.

Sutter, M. R. (1996). What do we know about the job and career satisfaction of secondary school assistant principals? *NASSP, 80,* 108–111.

Thompson, J. (1967). *Organizations in action.* New York: McGraw-Hill.

Tillman, L. C. (2003). From rhetoric to reality? Educational administration and the lack of racial and ethnic diversity within the profession. *University Council for Educational Administration Review, 45,* 1–4.

Tillman, L. C. (2004). (Un)intended consequences?: The impact of the Brown v. Board of Education decision on the employment status of Black educators. *Education and Urban Society, 36,* 280–303.

Tillman, L. C. (in press). Bringing the gifts that our ancestors gave: Continuing the legacy of excellence in African American school leadership. In J. Jackson (Ed.), *Strengthening the educational pipeline for African Americans: Informing policy and practice.* Albany: State University of New York Press.

Turner, R. H. (1960). Sponsored and contest mobility and the school system. *American Sociological Review, 25,* 855–867.

Tyack, D., & Hansot, E. (1982). *Managers of virtue: Public school leadership in America, 1890–1980.* New York: Basic Books.

U.S. Department of Education, National Center for Education Statistics, Schools and Staffing Survey. 1987–88 (administrator questionnaire), 1990–91 (administrator questionnaires), 1993–94 (principal questionnaires). Washington, DC: Author.

University Council for Educational Administration. (2003). *What we know about successful school leadership.* Retrieved March 25, 2005, from www.cepa.gse .rutgers.edu

Valverde, L. (1974). *Succession socialization: Its influence on school administrative candidates and its implications to the exclusion of minorities from administration.* Washington, DC: National Institute of Education.

Valverde, L. (1980). Promotion socialization: The informal process in large urban districts and its adverse effects on non-whites and women. *Journal of Educational Equity and Leadership, 1(1),* 36–46.

Valverde, L. (1987). Principals embracing cultural reality. *Teacher Education & Practice, (4)1,* 47–51.

Vollmer, H. M., & Mills, D. L. (Eds.). (1966). *Professionalization.* Englewood Cliffs, NJ: Prentice-Hall.

Waskiewicz, Peter. (1999). *Variables that contribute to job satisfaction of secondary school assistant principals.* Unpublished doctoral dissertation, Virginia Polytechnic Institute and State University, Blacksburg.

Weatherley, R., & Lipsky, M. (1977). Street-level bureaucrats and institutional innovation: Implementing special-education reform. *Harvard Educational Review, 47(2),* 171–197.

Weick, K. E. (1982). Management of organizational change among loosely coupled elements. In P. S. Goodman, et al. (Eds.), *Change in organizations.* San Francisco: Jossey-Bass.

Weiler, K. (1988). *Women teaching for change—Gender, class & power.* South Hadley, MA: Bergin & Garvey Publishers.

Winter, P. A., & Partenheimer, P. R. (2002). *Applicant attraction to assistant principal jobs: An experimental assessment.* Paper presented at the annual meeting of the University Council of Educational Administration (UCEA), Pittsburgh, PA. (ERIC Document Reproduction Service No. ED471558)

Wissler, D. F. (1984). *Hawthorne revisited: An alternative organizational model.* Mentone, CA: Greenspot.

Wissler, D. F., & Ortiz, F. I. (1988). *The superintendent's leadership in school reform.* New York: Falmer.

Wolcott, H. F. (1973). *The man in the principal's office: An ethnography.* New York: Holt, Rinehart & Winston.

Wynn, S. (2003). *Leadership skilled women teachers who say no to school administration: A case of career choice or career constraint?* Unpublished doctoral dissertation, University of North Carolina, Chapel Hill.

Young, M. D., & Skrla, L. (Eds.). (2003). *Reconsidering feminist research in educational leadership.* Albany: State University of New York Press.

Zellner, L., Jinkins, D., Gideon, B., Doughty, S., & McNamara, P. (2002). *Saving the principal: The evolution of initiatives that made a difference in the recruitment and retention of school leadership.* Paper presented at the annual meeting of the American Educational Research Association, New Orleans, LA. (ERIC Document Reproduction Service No. ED467670)

Index

186

**CORWIN
PRESS**

The Corwin Press logo—a raven striding across an open book—represents the union of courage and learning. Corwin Press is committed to improving education for all learners by publishing books and other professional development resources for those serving the field of PreK–12 education. By providing practical, hands-on materials, Corwin Press continues to carry out the promise of its motto: **"Helping Educators Do Their Work Better."**